All's Well That Ends Well. Edited by W. Osborne Brigstocke

THE ARDEN SHAKESPEARE
GENERAL EDITOR: W. J. CRAIG

ALL'S WELL THAT ENDS WELL

THE WORKS
OF
SHAKESPEARE

ALL'S WELL THAT ENDS WELL

EDITED BY

W. OSBORNE BRIGSTOCKE

METHUEN AND CO.
36 ESSEX STREET: STRAND
LONDON
1904

PR
2801
A2B7
cop.2

CONTENTS

	PAGE
INTRODUCTION	ix
ALL'S WELL THAT ENDS WELL	1

INTRODUCTION

All's Well that Ends Well, first published in the folio of 1623, is certainly one of the worst printed plays in the volume. It teems with obscure and corrupt passages, some of which, in spite of the erudition and ingenuity of generations of Shakespeare scholars, are still unexplained. There is almost unlimited scope for conjecture; consequently, one of the main difficulties is the sifting of endless emendations. I have throughout endeavoured to be as conservative of the original folio text as possible, relying rather on the reading of the first folio than on the versions of the other three, adopting subsequent emendations or conjectures only when supported by what seemed to me conclusive arguments. It seems preferable to leave doubtful readings as they are in the original; for conjectural corrections, unless quite indispensable, are best confined to the footnotes.

With regard to the carelessness of the printing, Hudson says that "it may be worth the while to observe . . . that in respect of plot and action the piece is of a somewhat forbidding, not to say repulsive, nature; and though it abounds in wisdom and is not wanting in poetry, and has withal much choice delineation of character, and contains scenes which stream down with the poet's raciest English, yet it is not among the plays which readers are often drawn to by mere recollections of delight; . . . the poet may have left the manuscript in a more unfinished and illegible state, from a sense of something ungenial and unattractive in the subject-matter and action of the play."[1] Perhaps: but surely the fact that the play is supposed to have been remodelled after the lapse of several years is hardly in keeping with the idea that Shakespeare saw something ungenial in the subject-matter. On the contrary, all seems to lead us to suppose that Shakespeare liked the subject sufficiently well to revise the greater part of an old comedy he had written years before, and also to treat of the same subject in *Measure for Measure*. Be that as it may, the play certainly does, as Dr. Hudson says, abound in wisdom and contain scenes which stream down with the poet's raciest English.

The data we possess for determining the time of composition are lamentably scant. Of direct, certain evidence there is none; neither external nor internal. *All's Well that Ends Well* is mentioned neither by contemporary theatre-goers nor in the Registers. In the piece itself there is nothing to point conclusively to a definite period—or rather, there are many things which point to different periods. Certainly not much to go upon.

In Meres's *Palladis Tamia* there is the mention of a play called *Love's Labour's Wonne*. Though Halliwell is of the opinion that this play has been lost, most critics agree that, considering the commercial value of Shakespeare's name, it is hardly likely that such a thing can have happened. If we possess the play at all, it is evident that we must have it under a different title. There are three plays which may

[1] Hudson, *Shakespeare: His Life, Art, and Characters*, vol. i. p. 374.

not unreasonably be called tales of "love's labour's won," namely, *The Tempest*, *The Taming of the Shrew*, and *All's Well that Ends Well*. This is not the place to discuss the several claims of these three plays: the battle has been fought out, and critics are now almost unanimous in declaring that *All's Well that Ends Well* is, in all probability, the play that Meres calls *Love's Labour's Wonne*;—a conclusion first arrived at by Dr. Farmer in his Essay on the Learning of Shakespeare (1767).

This would not only prove that the play must already have been written by the year 1598; it would also lead one to suppose that it was written in connection with *Love's Labour's Lost*—either before or shortly after it, as a sequel —presumably the latter, as *Love's Labour's Lost* is one of the very earliest plays we possess. That being so, 1590 might be taken to be the date of the first composition. *Love's Labour's Lost* was published in 1598, "newly corrected and augmented"; and it is possible that the companion play, though not published, may have undergone a similar correction about that time.

In the play itself we cannot find much to help us. There are one or two passages which lead Stokes to believe that Shakespeare may possibly (and it is just within the bounds of possibility that he may) have made use of the following works:—Tom Drum's Vants (etc.) in *Gentle Craft* (ii. 8), 1598; Mendoza's *Theorique and Practice of Warre* (IV. iii. 160-165), translated by Holy 1597; Nash's novel, *The Unfortunate Traveller, or Life of Jack Wilton*, 1594. Another passage (V. iii. 83-87) seems to Elze to refer to the gift of a ring by Elizabeth to Essex when he departed for Cadiz in 1596. He writes: "The circumstance of the ring is strangely not referred to till this last scene; and may have been introduced into the fifth act, at a remodelling in 1597, say, when Shakespeare would know of the Essex incident."[1]

The style and diction of a play are, as a rule, most useful in determining the period of composition; but in *All's Well that Ends Well* it is rather a stumbling-block than a help; for distinguished and learned critics have assigned dates ranging from 1590 to 1606, and where they have failed it is hardly likely that anyone can have success.

Elze thinks that "the unmistakable beauties of composition and characterisation" are indications that the piece cannot have been written very early. Though Helen's letter is written in sonnet form and though the Italian style is still prominent, he considers that it is certainly less pronounced than in the very early work. Rhyme is fairly abundant, and the clown is not furnished with all the proverbs and snatches of song which are characteristic of the clown of Shakespeare's later period. I gather from this that Elze would agree with Drake, who gives 1598, or with Chalmers, who gives 1599. Ulrici thinks the peculiar diction a sign of early composition, and gives 1590-1593; Hertzberg, on the other hand, thinks that this peculiar diction clearly indicates a late date of composition, say 1603; and he dismisses the idea that the play may have been written at two different periods. Malone at first conjectured 1598, and subsequently changed his mind and said 1606. Knight holds that there is no proof that it was

[1] Halliwell-Phillipps thinks that Shakespeare may have seen Deloney's second part of the *Gentle Craft* (1598), and taken from it the incidents of the Parolles story. See *Essays on Shakespeare*, Karl Elze, tr. L. D. Schmitz (1874), p. 147.

written after 1590. Though Delius emphatically asserts that the characteristic peculiarities of this play are in no way connected with the characteristic peculiarities of Shakespeare's early plays, Gervinus and v. Friesen are in favour of the theory that the play was written early and subsequently revised. The former writes: "The rhymed passages, the alternate rhymes, the sonnet letter of Helena, point to the form which the piece probably more uniformly bore, when with its first title it was placed by the side of *Love's Labour's Lost*, to the style of which those passages nearly correspond. By far the greatest part of the play, however, must have undergone . . . remodelling, for the prose-scenes, the soliloquies, which in profound thought and force often call to mind *Hamlet* and *Timon*, and challenge all the interpreter's art of arrangement, punctuation, and transposition, the comic passages, which in substance and form recall the scenes of Falstaff, all evidently belong to the later period of the poet's writing; [probably to] the years 1605 or 1606."[1] It was also Coleridge's decided opinion that *All's Well that Ends Well* was written at two different and rather distant periods of the poet's life, and Verplanck, who is of the same opinion, writes: "The contrast of two different modes of thought and manners of expression here mixed in the same piece, must be evident to all who have made the shades and gradations of Shakespeare's varying and progressive taste and mind at all the subject of study. Much of the graver dialogue, especially in the first two acts, reminds the reader in taste of composition, in rhythm and in a certain quaintness of ex-

---

[1] Gervinus, *Commentaries* (*All's Well* . . .), Eng. trans. by Bunnett, ed. 1863, vol. ii. p. 241, lines 10-22.

pression of *The Two Gentlemen of Verona*. On the other hand, there breaks forth everywhere, and in many cases entirely predominates, a grave moral thoughtfulness, expressed in a solemn, reflective and sometimes in a sententious levity of phrase and harshness of rhythm which seem to me to stamp many passages as belonging to the epoch of *Measure for Measure* or *King Lear*. We miss, too, the gay and fanciful imagery which shows itself continually alike amidst the passion and the moralising of the previous comedies."[1] Hudson closes his remarks on this question as follows: "To my taste, the better parts of the workmanship relish strongly of the poet's later style—perhaps I should say quite as strongly as the poorer parts do of its earlier. This would bring the revisal down to as late a time as 1603 or 1604: which date accords, not only with my own sense of the matter, but with the much better judgment of the critics I have quoted. I place the finished *Hamlet* at or near the close of the poet's middle period; and I am tolerably clear that in this play he discovers a mind somewhat more advanced in concentrated fulness, and a hand somewhat more practised in sinewy sternness than in the finished *Hamlet*."[2]

Thus, in spite of the undoubted difficulties due to the frequent changes of metre, style, and language, and in spite of the much more questionable inconsistency in dramatic power and moral tone, there are many weighty supporters of the theory that *All's Well that Ends Well* was written early and remodelled later; that there are clearly two

---

[1] I have retained this quotation, although I cannot give the exact reference. I cannot vouch for it; but I have no reason to suspect that the passage does not convey Verplanck's opinion.
[2] *Shakespeare: His Life, Art, and Characters*, ed. 1872, p. 377, lines 12-23.

INTRODUCTION

distinct styles, the one reminding one of the earliest plays, the other of the great plays of the period of tragedy; that the fourfold recurrence of the proverb "All's well that ends well" in the text of the play, and the apparent blending of the two titles in "All is well ended, if this suit be won," are strong circumstantial evidence in favour of accepting Dr. Farmer's conjecture that *All's Well that Ends Well* is the play mentioned by Meres in his *Palladis Tamia* under the name *Love's Labour's Wonne*; and lastly, that the faulty passages, which have baffled everyone, may be accounted for by supposing them to mark the places where the old and new versions were joined, and their obscurity to be due either to new passages being omitted or else inserted in the wrong place.

Everyone who reads this play is at first shocked and perplexed by the revolting idea which underlies the plot. It *is* revolting, there is no doubt about it; and it leaves so unpleasant a flavour with some people that it is not tasted again. I hold that the taste for *All's Well that Ends Well* is an acquired taste: and when the taste has once been acquired, one wonders how the revolting side of the plot could ever have hidden the manifold, and in certain respects unique, interest of the play. I say unique, because in no other play, so far as I know, do we have so curious a blending of Shakespeare's various styles; here a passage of florid rhetoric characteristic of the earliest work, here a phrase which seems a bettered version of some lines in *King John*, and there gleams of irony that surely come reflected from the dark period of *King Lear, Measure for Measure,* or *Hamlet.* Furthermore, the eye in time becomes accustomed to the brightness of Helen's personality, and recognises round her a number of lesser characters, unnoticed before. By studying to understand what Shakespeare added to the authentic story, we may come to conjecture why the tale of Helen's labours touched him, and in what spirit he intended us to read his rendering of it.

The story on which the play is founded forms Nov. 9, Giorn. iii. of the *Decameron*. Shakespeare must have read it in Paynter's version (*Palace of Pleasure*, 4to, 1566), for it can hardly be a coincidence that both English writers call the people of Sienna " the Senois." Paynter's " version of the tale of Giglietta di Nerbona is faithful, and that seems to have been the principal excellence at which he aimed: he . . . seems generally satisfied with the first word that presented itself to his mind, if it conveyed sufficiently the meaning of his author."[1] This is his version of Boccaccio's novel :—

" *Giletta a phisician's doughter of Narbon, healed the Frenche Kyng of a fistula, for reward whereof she demaunded Beltramo Counte of Rossiglione to husbande. The Counte beyng maried againste his will, for despite fled to Florence and loved an other. Giletta his wife, by pollicie founde meanes to lye with her husbande, in place of his lover, and was begotten with child of two soonnes: which knowen to her husbande, he received her againe, and afterwardes he lived in greate honor and felicitie.*

" In Fraunce there was a gentleman called Isnardo, the Counte of Rossiglione, who bicause he was sickly and diseased, kepte alwaies in his house a phisicion, named maister Gerardo of Narbona. This counte had one onely

[1] Payne Collier, "Shakespeare's Library," 1843, vol. ii.

sonne called Beltramo, a verie yonge childe, pleasaunt and faire. With whom there was nourished and broughte up, many other children of his age: emonges whom one of the doughters of the said phisicion, named Giletta, who ferventlie fill in love with Beltramo, more then was meete for a maiden of her age. This Beltramo, when his father was dedde, and left under the roial custodie of the Kyng, was sente to Paris, for whose departure the maiden was very pensive. A little while after, her father beyng likewise dedde, she was desirous to goe to Paris, onely to see the younge counte, if for that purpose she could gette any good occasion. But beyng diligently looked unto by her kinsfolke (bicause she was riche and fatherless) she could see no conviente waie for her intended journey: and being now mariageable, the love she bare to the counte was never out of her remembraunce, and she refused many husbandes with whom her kinsfolke would have placed her, without making them privie to the occasion of her refusall. Now it chaunced that she burned more in love with Beltramo than ever she did before, bicause she heard tell that hee was growen to the state of a goodly yonge gentlemanne. She heard by report, that the Frenche Kyng had a swellyng upon his breast, whiche by reason of ill cure was growen to a fistula, and did putte him to merveilous pain and grief, and that there was no phisicion to be founde (although many were proved) that could heale it, but rather did impaire the grief and made it worsse and worsse. Wherfore the Kyng, like one that was in dispaire, would take no more counsaill or helpe. Whereof the yonge maiden was wonderfull glad, and thought to have by this meanes, not onelie a lawfull occasion to goe to Paris, but if the disease were suche (as she supposed) easely to bryng to passe that she might have the Counte Beltramo to her husbande. Whereupon with such knowledge as she had learned at her fathers handes before time, shee made a pouder of certain herbes, which she thought meete for that disease, and rode to Paris. And the first thing she went about when she cam thither was to see the Counte Beltramo. And then she repaired to the Kyng, praying his grace to vouchsafe to shewe her his disease. The Kyng perceivyng her to be a faire yonge maiden and a comelie, would not hide it, but opened the same unto her. So soone as she sawe it, shee putte hym in comforte, that she was able to heale hym, saiyng: 'Sire, if it shall please your grace, I trust in God without any paine or grief unto your highness, within eighte daies I will make you whole of this disease.' The Kyng hearyng her saie so, began to mocke her, saiyng: 'How is it possible for thee, beyng a yong woman, to doe that which the best renouned phisicions in the worlde can not?' He thanked her for her good will, and made her a directe answere, that he was determined no more to followe the counsaile of any phisicion. Whereunto the maiden answered: 'Sire, you dispise my knowledge bicause I am yonge and a woman, but I assure you that I doe not minister phisicke by profession, but by the aide and helpe of God: and with the cunnyng of maister Gerardo of Narbona, who was my father, and a phisicion of greate fame so longe as he lived.' The Kyng hearyng those wordes, saied to hymself: 'This woman, peradventure, is sent unto me of God, and therefore why should I disdain to prove her cunnyng? sithens she promiseth to heale me within a litle space, without any offence or grief unto me.' And beyng determined to prove her, he said:

INTRODUCTION

'Damosell, if thou doest not heale me, but make me to breake my determinacion, what wilt thou shall folowe thereof.' 'Sire,' saied the maiden: 'Let me be kept in what guarde and kepyng you list: and if I dooe not heale you within these eight daies, let me bee burnte: but if I doe heale your grace what recompence shall I have then?' To whom the Kyng answered: 'Bicause thou art a maiden and unmarried, if thou heale me accordyng to thy promisse, I wil bestowe thee upon some gentleman, that shalbe of right good worship and estimacion.' To whom she answered: 'Sire, I am verie well content that you bestowe me in mariage: but I will have suche a husbande as I my self shall demaunde, without presumption to any of your children or other of your bloudde.' Which requeste the Kyng incontinently graunted. The yong maiden began to minister her phisicke, and in shorte space before her appoincted tyme, she had throughly cured the Kyng. And when the Kyng perceived himself whole, said unto her: 'Thou hast well deserved a husbande (Giletta) even suche a one as thy selfe shalt chose.' 'I have then my lorde (quod she) deserved the Countie Beltramo of Rossiglione, whom I have loved from my youthe.' The Kyng was very lothe to graunte hym unto her: but bicause he had made a promis which he was lothe to breake, he caused hym to be called forthe, and saied unto hym: 'Sir counte, bicause you are a gentleman of greate honour, our pleasure is, that you retourne home to your owne house, to order your estate according to your degree: and that you take with you a damosell which I have appoincted to be your wife.' To whom the counte gave his humble thankes, and demaunded what she was? 'It is she (quoth the Kyng) that with her medicines hath healed me.' The counte knewe her well, and had alreadie seen her, although she was faire, yet knowing her not to be of a stocke convenable to his nobilitie, disdainfullie said unto the King, 'Will you then (sir) give me a phisicion to wife? It is not the pleasure of God that ever I should in that wise bestowe my self.' To whom the Kyng said: 'Wilt thou then, that we should breake our faithe, which we to recover healthe have given to the damosell, who for a rewarde thereof asked thee to husband?' 'Sire (quoth Beltramo) you maie take from me al that I have, and give my persone to whom you please, bicause I am your subject: but I assure you I shall never be contented with that mariage.' 'Well you shall have her, (saied the Kyng) for the maiden is faire and wise, and loveth you moste intirely: thinkyng verelie you shall leade a more joyfull life with her, then with a ladie of a greater house.' The counte therewithal helde his peace, and the King made great preparacion for the mariage. And when the appoincted daie was come, the counte in the presence of the Kyng (although it were against his will) maried the maiden, who loved hym better then her owne self. Whiche dooen, the counte determinyng before what he would doe, praied licence to retourne to his countrie to consummat the mariage. And when he was on horsebacke he went not thither, but tooke his journey into Thuscane, where understandyng that the Florentines and Senois were at warres, he determined to take the Florentines parte, and was willinglie received and honourablie interteigned, and made capitaine of a certaine nomber of men, continuyng in their service a longe tyme. The newe maried gentlewoman, scarce contented with that, and hopyng by her well doyng to cause hym to

INTRODUCTION

retourne into his countrie, went to Rossiglione, where she was received of all his subjectes for their ladie. And perceivyng that through the countes absence all thinges were spoiled and out of order, she like a sage lady, with greate diligence and care, disposed all thynges in order againe; whereof the subjectes rejoysed verie much, bearyng to her their hartie love and affection, greatlie blamyng the counte bicause he could not contente himself with her. This notable gentlewoman having restored all the countrie againe, sent worde thereof to the counte her husbande, by two knightes of the countrie, whiche she sent to signifie unto hym, that if it were for her sake that he had abandoned his countrie, he should sende her worde thereof, and she to doe hym pleasure, would depart thence. To whom he chorlishlie saied: 'Lette her doe what she list: for I doe purpose to dwell with her, when she shall have this ryng (meanyng a ryng which he wore) upon her finger, and a soonne in her armes begotten by me.' He greatly loved that ryng, and kepte it verie carefullie, and never tooke it of from his finger, for a certaine vertue that he knewe it had. The knightes hearyng the harde condicion of twoo thinges impossible: and seyng that by them he could not be removed from his determinacion, thei retourned againe to the ladie, tellinge her his answere: who, verie sorrowfull, after she hadde a good while bethought herself, purposed to finde meanes to attaine to those twoo thynges, to the intente that thereby she might recover her husbande. And havyng advised with her self what to doe, she assembled the noblest and chiefest of her countrie, declaring unto them in lamentable wise what shee had alredie dooen, to winne the love of the counte, shewyng them also what followed thereof. And in the ende saied unto them, that she was lothe the counte for her sake should dwell in perpetuall exile: therefore she determined to spende the rest of her tyme in pilgrimages and devocion, for preservacion of her soule, praiyng them to take the charge and governmente of the countrie, and that they would lette the counte understande, that she had forsaken his house, and was removed farre from thence: with purpose never to retourne to Rossiglione againe. Many teares were shedde by the people, as she was speakyng these wordes, and divers supplications were made unto him to alter his opinion, but al in vaine. Wherefore commending them all unto God, she tooke her waie with her maide, and one of her kinsemen, in the habite of a pilgrime, well furnished with silver and precious jewelles: tellyng no man whither shee wente, and never rested till she came to Florence: where arrivyng by fortune at a poor widowes house, she contented her self with the state of a poore pilgrime, desirous to here newes of her lorde, whom by fortune she sawe the next daie passing by the house (where she lay) on horsebacke with his companie. And although she knewe him well enough, yet she demaunded of the good wife of the house what he was: who answered that he was a straunge gentleman, called the counte Beltramo of Rossiglione, a curteous knighte, and wel beloved in the citie, and that he was mervellously in love with a neighbor of hers, that was a gentlewoman, verie poore and of small substaunce, neverthelesse of right honest life and report, and by reason of her povertie was yet unmarried, and dwelte with her mother, that was a wise and honest ladie. The countess well notyng these wordes, and by litle and litle debatyng every particular point thereof, comprehendyng the effecte of those newes, concluded what to doe, and when she had well understanded whiche was the house, and the name of the ladie, and of her doughter that was beloved of the counte: upon a daie repaired to the house secretlie in the habite of a pilgrime, where finding the mother and doughter in poore estate emonges their familie, after she hadde saluted them, tolde the mother that she had to saie unto her. The gentlewoman risyng up, curteouslie interteigned her, and beyng entred alone into a chamber, thei satte doune, and the countesse began to saie unto her in this wise. 'Madame we thinke that ye be one upon whom fortune doeth frowne, so well as upon me: but if you please, you maie bothe comfort me and your self.' The ladie answered, 'That there was nothyng in the worlde whereof she was more desirous then of honest comforte.' The countesse procedyng in her talke, saied unto her: 'I have nede now of your fidelitie and trust, whereupon if I doe staie, and you deceive mee, you shall bothe undoe me and your self.' 'Tel me then what it is hardelie (saied the gentlewoman:) if it bee your pleasure: for you shall never bee deceived of me.' Then the countesse begaune to recite her whole estate of love: tellyng her what she was, and what had chaunced to that present daie, in such perfite order that the gentlewoman belevyng her woordes, bicause she had partlie heard report thereof before, begaune to have compassion upon her, and after that the countesse had rehearsed all the whole circumstaunce, she continued her purpose, saying: 'Now you have heard emonges other my troubles, what twoo thynges thei bee, whiche behoveth me to have, if I do recover my husbande, which I knowe none can helpe me to obtain, but onely you, if it bee true that I heare, which is, that the counte my husbande, is farre in love with your doughter.' To whom the gentlewoman saied: 'Madame, if the counte love my doughter, I knowe not, albeit the likelihoode is greate: but what am I able to doe, in that which you desire?' 'Madame,' answered the countesse, 'I will tell you: but first I will declare what I mean to doe for you, if my determinacion be brought to effect: I see your faier doughter of good age, redie to marie, but as I understand the cause why she is unmarried, is the lacke of substance to bestowe upon her. Wherfore I purpose, for recompense of the pleasure, which you shall dooe for me, to give so much redie money to marie her honorably, as you shall thinke sufficient.' The countesse' offer was very well liked of the ladie, bicause she was but poore: yet having a noble hart, she said unto her, 'Madame, tell me wherein I maie do you service: and if it be a thing honest, I will gladlie performe it, and the same being brought to passe, do as it shal please you.' Then saied the countesse: 'I thinke it requisite, that by some one whom you trust, that you give knowledge to the counte my husbande, that your doughter is, and shalbe at his commaundement: and to the intent she maie bee well assured that he loveth her in deede above any other, that she praieth him to sende her a ring that he weareth upon his finger, whiche ring she heard tell he loved verie derely: and when he sendeth the ryng, you shall give it unto me, and afterwardes sende hym woorde, that your doughter is redie to accomplishe his pleasure, and then you shall cause him secretly to come hither, and place me by hym (in steede of your doughter) peradventure God will give me the grace, that I maie bee with childe, and so havyng this ryng on my finger, and the childe in myne armes begotten by him, I shall recover him, and by your meanes continue with hym, as a wife ought to doe with her husbande.' This thing seemed difficulte unto the gentlewoman: fearyng that there would followe reproche unto her doughter. Notwithstandyng, consideryng what an honest parte it were, to be a meane that the good ladie should recover her husband, and that she should doe it for a good purpose, havyng affiaunce in her honest affection, not onely promised the countesse to bryng this to passe, but in fewe daies with greate subtiltie, folowyng the order wherein she was instructed, she had gotten the ryng, although it was with the countes ill will, and toke order that the countesse in stede of her doughter did lye with hym. And at the first meetyng, so affectuously desired by the counte: God so disposed the matter that the countesse was begotten with child, of twoo goodly sonnes, and her delivery chaunced at the due time. Whereupon the gentlewoman, not onely contented the countesse at that tyme with the companie of her husbande, but at many other times so secretly that it was never knowen: the counte not thinkyng that he had lien with his wife, but with her whom he loved. To whom at his uprisyng in the mornyng, he used many curteous and amiable woordes, and gave divers faire and precious jewelles, whiche the countesse kepte most carefullie: and when shee perceived herself with childe, she determined no more to trouble the gentlewoman, but saied unto her, 'Madame, thankes be to God and you, I have the thyng that I desire, and even so it is tyme to recompence your desert, that afterwardes I maie departe.' The gentlewoman saied unto her, that if she had doen any pleasure agreable to her mind, she was right glad thereof whiche she did, not for hope of rewarde, but because it apperteined to her by well doyng so to doe. Whereunto the countesse saied: 'Your saiyng pleaseth me well, and likewise for my parte, I dooe not purpose to give unto you the thing you shall demaunde of me in rewarde, but for consideracion of your well doyng, which duetie forceth me to so dooe.' The gentlewoman then constrained with necessitie, demaunded of her with greate bashfulnesse, an hundred poundes to marie her doughter. The countesse perceivyng the shamefastnesse of the gentlewoman, and hearyng her curteous demaunde, gave her five hundred poundes, and so many faire and costly jewels whiche almoste amounted to like valer. For whiche the gentlewoman more then contented, gave most hartie thankes to the countesse, who departed from the gentlewoman and retourned to her lodging. The gentlewoman to take occasion from the counte of any farther repaire, or sendyng to her house, tooke her doughter with her, and went into the countrie to her frendes. The counte Beltramo, within fewe daies after, beyng revoked home to his owne house by his subjectes, (hearyng that the countesse was departed from thence) retourned. The countesse knowynge that her husband was gone from Florence and retourned into his countrie, was verie glad and contented, and she continewed in Florence till the tyme of her child-bedde was come, and was brought a bedde of twoo soones, which were verie like unto their father, and caused them carefullie to be noursed and brought up, and when she sawe tyme, she toke her journey (unknowen to any manne) and arrived at Montpellier, and restyng her self there for certaine daies, hearyng newes of the counte, and where he was, and that upon the daie of All Sainctes, he purposed to make a great feast and assemblie of ladies and knightes, in her pilgrimes weede she wente thither. And knowyng that thei were all assembled, at the palace of the counte, redie to sitte doune at the table, she passed through the people without change of apparell, with her twoo sonnes in her armes: and when she was come up into the hall, even to the place where the counte was, fallyng doune prostrate at his feete, wepyng, saied unto him: 'My lorde, I am thy poor infortunate wife, who to the intent thou mightest returne and dwel in thine owne house, have been a great while beggyng about the worlde. Therefore I now beseche thee, for the honour of God, that thou wilt observe the condicions, whiche the twoo knightes (that I sent unto thee) did commaunde me to doe: for beholde, here in myne armes, not onelie one sonne begotten by thee, but twaine, and likewise thy rynge. It is now tyme then (if thou kepe promis) that I should be received as thy wife.' The counte hearyng this, was greatly astonned, and knewe the rynge and the children also, thei were so like hym. 'But tell me (quod he) how is this come to passe?' The countesse to the great admiracion of the counte, and of all those that were in presence, rehearsed unto them in order all that, whiche had been doen, and the whole discourse thereof. For whiche cause the counte knowyng the thynges she had spoken to be true (and perceivyng her constaunt minde and good witte, and the twoo faier yonge boies to kepe his promise made, and to please his subjectes, and the ladies that made sute unto him, to accept her from that time forthe as his lawfull wife, and to honour her) abjected his obstinate rigour: causyng her to rise up, and imbraced and kissed her, acknowledgyng her againe for his lawfull wife. And after he had apparelled her according to her estate, to the greate pleasure and contentacion of those that were there, and of all his other frendes not onelie that daie, but many others, he kepte great chere, and from that tyme forthe, he loved and honoured her, as his dere spouse and wife."

It was from this uncouth version of the story that Shakespeare drew inspiration for Helena—according to Coleridge "his loveliest creation." Mrs. Jameson tells us that "in Helena we have a . . . character . . . allied, indeed, to Juliet as a picture of fervent, enthusiastic, self-forgetting love, but differing wholly from her in other respects; for Helen is the union of strength of passion with strength of character . . . a character almost as difficult to delineate in fiction as to find in real life . . . touched with the most soul-subduing pathos and developed with the most consummate skill.

"Helena, as a woman, is more passionate than imaginative; and, as a character, she bears the same relation to Juliet that Isabel bears to Portia. There is equal unity of purpose and effect, with much less of the glow of imagery and the external colouring of poetry in the sentiments, language, and details. It is passion developed under its most profound and serious aspect; as in Isabella we have the serious and the thoughtful, not the brilliant side of intellect. Both Helena and Isabel are distinguished by high mental powers, tinged with a melancholy sweetness; but in Isabella the serious and energetic part of the character is founded in religious principle, in Helena it is founded in deep passion.

"There never was, perhaps, a more beautiful picture of a woman's love, cherished in secret, not self-consuming in silent languishment—not pining in thought—not passive and 'desponding over its idol'—but patient and hopeful, strong in its own intensity, and sustained by its own fond faith. The passion here reposes upon itself for all its interest; it derives nothing from art or ornament or circumstance; it has nothing of the picturesque charm or glowing romance of Juliet; nothing of the poetical splendour of Portia or the vestal grandeur of Isabel. The situation of Helena is the most painful and degrading in which a woman can be placed. She is poor and lowly: she loves a man who is far her superior in rank, who repays her love with indifference, and rejects her hand with scorn. She marries him against his will; he leaves her with contumely on the day of their marriage, and makes his return to her arms depend on conditions apparently impossible. All the circumstances and details with which Helena is surrounded are shocking to our feelings and wounding to our delicacy; and yet the beauty of the character is made to triumph over all; and Shakespeare, resting for all his effect on its internal resources and its genuine truth and sweetness, has not even availed himself of some extraneous advantages with which Helen is represented in the original story . . . Helena, in the play, derives no dignity or interest from place or circumstance, and rests for all our sympathy and respect solely upon the truth and intensity of her affections. She is, indeed, represented to us as one

>Whose beauty did astonish the survey
>Of richest eyes; whose words all ears took captive;
>Whose dear perfection hearts that scorn'd to serve
>Humbly call'd mistress.

As her dignity is derived from mental power, without any alloy of pride, so her humility has a peculiar grace ... She is more sensible to his greatness than to her own littleness: she is continually looking from herself up to him, not from him down to herself. She has been bred up under the same roof with him; she has adored him from infancy. Her love is not 'th' infection taken in at the eyes' nor kindled by youthful romance: it appears to have taken root in her being, to have grown with her years, and to have gradually absorbed all her thoughts and faculties, until her fancy 'carries no favour in it but Bertram's,' and 'there is no living, none, if Bertram be away.' ...

"And although Helena tells herself that she loves in vain, a conviction stronger than reason tells her that she does not: her love is like a religion, pure, holy, and deep: the blessedness to which she has lifted her thoughts is for ever before her; to despair would be a crime—it would be to cast herself away and die. The faith of her affection, combining with the natural energy of her character, believing all things possible, makes them so. It could say to the mountain of pride which stands between her and her hopes, 'Be thou removed!' and it is removed. This is the solution of her behaviour in the marriage scene, where Bertram, with obvious reluctance and disdain, accepts her hand, which the King, his feudal lord and guardian, forces on him. Her maidenly feeling is at first shocked, and she shrinks back—

> That you are well restor'd, my lord, I am glad:
> Let the rest go.

But shall she weakly relinquish the golden opportunity, and dash the cup from her lips at the moment it is presented? Shall she cast away the treasure for which she has ventured both life and honour, when it is just within her grasp? Shall she, after compromising her feminine delicacy by the public disclosure of her preference, be thrust back into shame, 'to blush out the remainder of her life,' and die a poor, lost, scorned thing? This would be very pretty and interesting, and characteristic in Viola or Ophelia, but not at all consistent with that high, determined spirit, that moral energy, with which Helena is portrayed. Pride is the only obstacle opposed to her. She is not despised and rejected as a woman, but as a poor physician's daughter; and this, to an understanding so clear, so strong, so just as Helena's, is not felt as an unpardonable insult. The mere pride of rank and birth is a prejudice of which she cannot comprehend the force, because her mind towers so immeasurably above it; and, compared to the infinite love which swells within her own bosom, it sinks into nothing. She cannot conceive that he to whom she has devoted her heart and truth, her soul, her life, her services, must not one day love her in return; and once her own beyond the reach of fate, that her cares, her caresses, her unwearied, patient tenderness, will not at last 'win her lord to look upon her'—

> ... For time will bring on summer,
> When briers shall have leaves as well as thorns,
> And be as sweet as sharp!

It is this fond faith which, hoping all things, enables her to endure all things; which hallows and dignifies the surrender of her woman's pride, making it a sacrifice on which virtue and love throw a mingled incense."[1]

[1] Mrs. Jameson, *Characteristics of Women* (Shakespeare's Heroines).

I cannot feel much sympathy for the elaborate German treatise in which "pride of rank" is held to be the vice ridiculed, the fact that "worth is rank" the moral of the play.[1] It seems preferable to avoid making each drama turn as it were on some central pivot: life does not move in that way. Any fragment of life may contain one or all of the ideas that German critics would prove to be singly the keynote of a play. May we not more profitably study to see what part of this life Shakespeare most clearly sympathises with, which runner is his favourite, what way of running evidently the one that seems best to him? No one denies that Shakespeare is as nearly impersonal as it is possible to be. But it is hardly possible for anyone to make a plain statement of facts, giving both sides of each case, without betraying his own opinion—if only by the wording of the phrases. Each play is essentially a statement of facts: and each play contains, at least to a certain degree, a statement of both sides of all questions. It is from this, and almost exclusively from this, that we must hope for reliable information regarding Shakespeare's theories of life. Professor Dowden writes: "The Elizabethan drama is thoroughly free from lassitude, and from that lethargy of heart, which most of us have felt at one time or another. . . . To this mood of barren world-weariness the Elizabethan drama comes with no direct teaching, but with a vision of life. Even though death end all, these things at least *are*—beauty and force, purity, sin, and love, and anguish and joy. These

---

[1] Gervinus, *Shakespeare Commentaries*, tr. Bunnett, 1863, vol. i. p. 252: "The idea, that merit goes before rank, has, as we shall presently see, expressly occupied Shakespeare's mind in the period before us."

things are, and therefore life cannot be a little idle whirl of dust. We are shown the strong man taken in the toils, the sinner sinking farther and farther away from light and reality and the substantial life of things into the dubious and the dusk, the pure heart all vital, and confident, and joyous; we are shown the glad, vicarious sacrifice of soul for soul, the malign activity of evil, the vindication of right by the true justiciary; we are shown the good common things of the world, and the good things that are rare; the love of parents and children, the comradeship of young men, the exquisite vivacity, courage and high-spirited intellect of noble girlhood, the devotion of man and woman to man and woman. The vision of life rises before us; and we know that the vision represents a reality."[1] And a reality looked at not in the light of its being transient, but as being of great value and worth fighting for. The Elizabethans of all men knew best how to value life and to make the most of it, and it is interesting to see what price the greatest of them puts on some things we might look upon as being useless. Not one of us but feels at first that Bertram is absolutely worthless, a rogue, a liar, and mean. It is significant that Shakespeare has intensified the moral failings of this man and made him more repulsive still by laying emphasis on his superficial attractiveness. There seems to be a hint of this at the very beginning (Act I. sc. i.), when the Countess says, "Where an unclean mind carries virtuous qualities, there commendations go with pity; they are virtues and traitors too"; though it must be confessed that Bertram's good

[1] *Shakespeare: His Mind and Art*, p. 30 *sq.*

qualities may be summed up by saying that he was handsome and brave.

> Youth, thou bear'st thy father's face;
> Frank nature, rather curious than in haste,
> Hath well composed thee. Thy father's moral parts
> Mayst thou inherit too!

But at that time Bertram had not inherited, as far as one could see, any of his father's moral parts—or if he had, they had grown viciously. Both contempt and bitterness were in his pride; his honour was not clock to itself, nor did he obey the hand of it; and, though he was born of so good a father, all went to demonstrate that Bertram was but a goer backward. He was one of those men who make a good impression—"Whatsome'er he is, he's bravely taken here," says Diana. But however much we despise Bertram, it is unnecessary to go to the length of saying that Helen's love for him is "a tragic perversion." Surely there are two most weighty arguments in his favour: Helen—"Shakespeare's loveliest creation"—thought him worth struggling for: and Shakespeare let him have her. Dr. Herford calls it irony. But Helena's wish to cure the King *seemed* rather tragic—and yet it proved successful; and, as Elze has pointed out, she cures Bertram as she cured the King. To the King she says:

> What is infirm from your sound parts shall fly,
> Health shall live free, and sickness freely die.

The same with Bertram. His disease was Parolles—a snipt-taffeta fellow, as the Countess describes him, whose villanous saffron would have made all the unbaked and doughy youth of a nation in his colour. Of him Bertram is rid when he accepts Helen. But Dr. Herford holds that Shakespeare had never yet pictured the tragic perversion of a maiden's passion, as he does here. He goes on to say: "It is a picture characteristic of the years when in *Julius Cæsar* and in *Hamlet* he was laying bare, with deepening irony, the fatalities which lie in wait for the weakness of noble characters. The issues are here less grave, but the irony is even more pronounced, in so far as Helen's passion for Bertram seems to spring not from any flaw in her clear and penetrating mind, but from something fundamentally irrational in the nature of love itself. Christian idealism sees the peculiar glory of love in its power of transcending and ignoring distinctions of merit and pouring itself forth on the mean and lowly. Modern Romanticism, from a kindred but distinct point of view, has delighted to picture the salvation of a worthless man by a woman's devoted love. But neither of these transcendent ways of looking at love is anywhere suggested in Shakespeare. Helen's love is an idolatry, and finds its highest expression in adoring self-subjection: yet the triumph of her love is merely external. Of the sequel we are left to form what ominous conjecture we may from the perfunctory declaration of the shrewd boggler in the last lines:

> If she, my liege, can make me know this clearly
> I'll love her dearly, ever, ever dearly."

That is one way of looking at the play. Of course the question of what "ominous conjectures" we are likely to make, is not one to argue. Some will agree with Dr. Herford and expect the worst. Others may prefer not to conjecture at all: they may find plenty to enjoy in the play, troubling themselves as little about what happened "ever, ever after" as the Elizabethans did, in practical life, about what was to happen in the "undiscovered country from whose bourne no traveller returns." Lastly, there may be some who think that the prospect is not so gloomy after all. To be sure, Bertram is indeed "haughty, rash and unbridled, assuming though ill-advised, influenced by the most wretched society, and entirely devoid of judgment and reflection." (Gervinus). But throughout there is a force of character which works in the opposite direction: Helen appears "humble, meek, modest, but perfectly mature, wise and prudent, endowed with high aspirations and instinctively impelled to follow them" (Gervinus). Is it not probable that the influence of Helen's clear purpose and resolute will (she has been called the antithesis to Hamlet); will end by giving Bertram's character the wisdom and the experience he so sorely stands in need of? It must have been a great shock to his pride to discover how entirely Parolles had duped him: and a still more wholesome lesson to him to learn how he had been deceived by Diana. Lafeu speaks contemptuously of him, and his words must have touched him to the quick. All the evil influence is taken from him: he has the guidance only of such friends as the King and his mother, besides an angel to bless him, unworthy husband that he is. The Countess declares that

> he cannot thrive
> Unless her prayers, whom heaven delights to hear
> And loves to grant, reprieve him from the wrath
> Of greatest justice.

May we not suppose that "all is well ended" because her prayers do reprieve him from the wrath of justice?

INTRODUCTION xxxvii

There is no Parolles in the original story. Elze suggests that he is meant to show us what Bertram may become if Helen does not succeed in wooing him, just as we see in the Countess what Helen will one day be like. He has been compared with Falstaff, which is not only irrelevant, but also a little unfair on our fat friend. The witty knight may justly disclaim any relationship to this cowardly liar. Parolles must rather be looked upon as the etymon of that Iago whose last words were

> From this time forth I never will speak word.

In *Othello* the "window of lattice" was not so easy to look through; it was so well shuttered that Desdemona, instead of being able to say, "one that goes with him . . . I *know* him," was left in ignorance,

> If any such there be, heaven pardon him . . .

so securely fastened that Othello did not "find" him until it was too late. All the terrible possibilities which lie in a man like Parolles if he happens to be not "a great way fool" were developed in Iago, a terrible incarnation of malice.

Shakespeare's Countess is a charming old lady: full of tenderest sympathy for the sweet girl she has, so to speak, adopted; she loves her as a daughter—and it is noticeable that one can hardly conceive of anyone else being able to be so kind and helpful to her. "Under the circumstances Helena's mother would not have been at all a fitting person to assist and encourage her love. The Countess was required, with her gentle disposition. She loves Helena for her purity, her honesty, her clear-sightedness, her modesty, her beauty; her love and esteem are increased the more Helena does to bring about her love's desire, until she loves her almost as much as her son" (Elze).

Lafeu, the steward, and the clown are also Shakespeare's own creations.

In Dr. Halliwell-Phillipps's notes on this play I find two passages which I venture to quote verbatim.

"It is worthy of remark that Shakespeare's comedy at a later period, seems to have passed under the name of *Monsieur Parolles*, that appellation being assigned to it by King Charles I. in a manuscript note in a copy of the second folio of 1632, preserved at Windsor Castle, which formerly belonged to that unfortunate monarch. No notice of *All's Well that Ends Well*, under that title, has been discovered of a date previous to its entry on the books of the Stationers' Company, in November 1623, where it is placed in the list of 'soe manie of the said copies as are not formerly entred to other men.'"

"No records of any early performance of *All's Well that Ends Well* has yet been discovered, and it does not appear to have been revived in the seventeenth century after the accession of Charles II., nor, indeed, until October 1741, when it was produced at Drury-lane theatre, Mrs. Woffington taking the part of Helena and Theophilus Cibber that of Parolles. It was again revived, under the superintendence of Garrick, in 1757, when Mrs. Prichard acted the Countess; Miss Macklin, Helen; Mrs. Davies, Diana; Woodward, Parolles; Berry, Lafeu; and Davies, the King. In the year 1785 it was altered by Frederic Pilon, reduced to three acts, and performed at the Haymarket theatre, but this version was not printed. The alteration in use at the theatres during the last sixty years is that by Kemble, in which the offensive peculiarities of the story are to a great extent concealed, and the principal condition in Bertram's letter entirely omitted. . . . It is scarcely a matter of surprise that the performance of the drama in this vitiated form, should not have met, at any recent period, with the success that it probably commanded on the Shakespearean stage."

Mr. P.-A. Daniel's time-analysis of this play is as follows:—

Day 1. Act I. sc. i.
 Interval. Bertram's journey to Court.
Day 2. Act I. sc. ii. and iii.
 Interval. Helena's journey to Court.
Day 3. Act II. sc. i. and ii.
 Interval, two days. Cure of the King's malady.
Day 4. Act II. sc. iii., iv., and v.
 Interval. Helena's return to Rousillon. Bertram's journey to Florence.
Day 5. Act III. sc. i. and ii.
Day 6. Act III. sc. iii. and iv.
 Interval, "some two months."
Day 7. Act III. sc. v.
Day 8. Act III. sc. vi. and vii., Act IV. sc. i. and ii.
Day 9. Act IV. sc. iii. and iv.
 Interval. Bertram's return to Rousillon. Helena's return to Marseilles.
Day 10. Act IV. sc. v., Act V. sc. i.
Day 11. Act V. sc. ii. and iii.

Total time about three months: eleven days represented on the stage.

INTRODUCTION

By the courtesy of the British Museum authorities I have been able to base the present text upon their copies of the folios. I have also had before me the *Cambridge Shakespeare*, invaluable to anyone who studies the text critically. I gained something from most of the editions I consulted, and it is therefore impossible to acknowledge my indebtedness more particularly. I have throughout endeavoured to mention my authority, whenever I knew the source of my information.

I am indebted to Mr. A. E. Thiselton's notes on the play; though I have not always been able to agree with his versions, his comments are excellent and in many ways most valuable. Professor Proescholdt has constantly aided me with criticisms and suggestions, and Mr. W. J. Craig, Editor of the *Oxford Shakespeare*, placed his large collection of manuscript notes at my disposal, and also the manuscript of his "Little Quarto Shakespeare." Any value that this edition may possess is entirely due to their generous assistance. I take this opportunity of expressing my thanks for this valuable assistance.

References to plays of Shakespeare other than *All's Well that Ends Well* are given with the numbering (etc.) of the Globe edition.

ALL'S WELL THAT ENDS WELL

DRAMATIS PERSONÆ[1]

KING OF FRANCE.
DUKE OF FLORENCE.
BERTRAM, *Count of Rousillon.*
LAFEU, *an old Lord.*
PAROLLES, *a Follower of Bertram.*
RINALDO, *Steward to the Countess of Rousillon.*
LAVACHE, *Clown, in her household.*
A Page.

COUNTESS OF ROUSILLON, *Mother to Bertram.*
HELENA, *a Gentlewoman protected by the Countess.*
A Widow of Florence.
DIANA, *Daughter to the Widow.*
VIOLENTA,[2] } *Neighbours and Friends to the Widow.*
MARIANA,

Lords, Officers, Soldiers, etc., French and Florentine.

SCENE: *Rousillon; Paris; Florence; Marseilles.*

---

[1] Dramatis Personæ] Not given in the 1623 F. First enumerated by Rowe.
[2] *Violenta*] a mute personage; retained because some have thought that Diana's first speech in III. v. may belong to her.

ALL'S WELL THAT ENDS WELL

ACT I

SCENE I.—*Rousillon. A Room in the Countess's Palace.*

Enter BERTRAM, *the* COUNTESS OF ROUSILLON, HELENA, *and* LAFEU, *all in black.*

Count. In delivering my son from me, I bury a second husband.

Ber. And I in going, madam, weep o'er my father's death anew; but I must attend his majesty's command, to whom I am now in ward, evermore 5 in subjection.

Laf. You shall find of the king a husband, madam; you, sir, a father. He that so generally is at all

---

3 *And I, in going, madam*] F 1; *And in going madam* F 2, 3; *And in going, madam, I* Rowe.

Rousillon] or Roussillon, an old province of France, separated from Spain by the Pyrenees. Perpignan was the capital, as it is of the modern department of Pyrénées-Orientales, which occupies nearly the same territory. (Rolfe.)

4. *attend*] be in attendance on; cf. "each hath his place and function to attend" (*1 Henry VI.* I. i. 173).

5. *in ward*] When the feudal lord of an estate died, the heir, if still a minor, became the ward of the sovereign, who often deputed some nobleman to "take the charge." The sovereign could even dispose of his ward's marriage.

7. *of the king*] Cf. "even such a husband Hast thou of me as she is for a wife" (*Merchant of Venice*, III. v. 89). "We shall find of him A shrewd contriver" (*Julius Cæsar*, II. i. 157).

8. *generally*] altogether. Cf. "This gentleman To whom we all rest generally beholding" (*Taming of the Shrew*, I. ii. 274).

times good, must of necessity hold his virtue to
you, whose worthiness would stir it up where it   10
wanted rather than lack it where there is such
abundance.

Count. What hope is there of his majesty's amend-
ment?

Laf. He hath abandoned his physicians, madam;   15
under whose practices he hath persecuted time
with hope, and finds no other advantage in the
process but only the losing of hope by time.

Count. This young gentlewoman had a father,—O,
that "had," how sad a passage 'tis!—whose skill   20

---

11. *lack*] *slack* Theobald (Warburton).   16. *persecuted*] *prosecuted* Hanmer.

---

9. *hold*] continue to devote. Cf. "I hold my duty, as I hold my soul, Both to my God and to my gracious king" (*Hamlet*, II. ii. 44).

10-12. *worthiness . . . abundance*] your worthiness is such that it would win "virtue" not only from a king at all times good, but even from one slow to kindly feeling.

11. *lack*] Theobald's proposal to substitute "slack" for "lack" seems good. The word in question is clearly in antithesis to "stir it up," and it is rather difficult to get much meaning out of "worthiness lacked it."

16, 17. *persecuted . . . hope*] Schmidt says: "not very intelligibly used." The meaning is: the king for a while hoped so fervently, that the idea of time was banished from his mind: he had, by the advice of his physicians, maltreated the present time and inflicted upon himself much pain in the hope of ultimately curing his disorder; time had, however, outlived the persecution and ended by quashing hope. Time=lifetime; cf. "out of thy long experienced time, Give me some counsel" (*Romeo and Juliet*, IV. i. 60). Mr. Thiselton (quoting Minshew) connects

"persecute" with "persequor." But is there anything to show that Shakespeare used "persecute" in its primary sense?

20. *that "had"*] Blackstone quotes the *Heautontimorumenos* of Terence, where Menedenus says:
"—Filium unicum adolescentulum
Habeo. Ah, quid dixi? habere
me? imo—habui, Chreme
Nunc habeam necne incertum est."
The same idea has been made use of by Dante, Spenser, and others.

20. *sad a passage*] "Passage is anything that passes. So we now say a passage of an author; and we used to say, the passages of a reign. When the Countess mentions Helena's loss of a father, she recollects her own loss of a husband, and stops to observe how heavily the word 'had' *passes* through her mind." This is Johnson's explanation. The word is a difficult one to understand. Dowden conjectures "occurrence," as in *Cymbeline*, III. iv. 94, "act of common passage." The word occurs again in *Comedy of Errors*, III. i. 99, "Now is the stirring passage of the day." Steevens quotes "two philosophers that jeer and weep at the passage

was almost as great as his honesty; had it
stretch'd so far, would have made nature immortal,
and death should have play for lack of work.
Would, for the king's sake, he were living! I
think it would be the death of the king's disease. 25
Laf. How called you the man you speak of, madam?
Count. He was famous, sir, in his profession, and it
was his great right to be so: Gerard de Narbon.
Laf. He was excellent indeed, madam: the king very
lately spoke of him admiringly, and mournfully. 30
He was skilful enough to have liv'd still, if know-
ledge could be set up against mortality.
Ber. What is it, my good lord, the king languishes of?
Laf. A fistula, my lord.
Ber. I heard not of it before. 35
Laf. I would it were not notorious. Was this gentle-
woman the daughter of Gerard de Narbon?
Count. His sole child, my lord; and bequeathed to
my overlooking. I have those hopes of her good
that her education promises; her dispositions she 40

22. *would*] *it would* Rowe, *'t would* Singer. 23. *have play*] *have had play*
Hanmer, *have play'd* Warburton. 40. *promises; her*] Rowe, *promises her*
Ff, *promises her;* Pope; *dispositions*] *disposition* Rowe.

of the world" in the English Intelli-
gencer, a tragi-comedy, 1641. The
word undoubtedly does mean "occurrence" very frequently. Steevens
quotes other instances where this meaning is perfectly evident. Nevertheless
I am inclined to prefer the explanation
that "passage" here means "passing
away." The word is so used by Shakespeare: "Would some part of my young
years Might but redeem the passage of
your age!" (*1 Henry VI.* II. v. 108).
"When he is fit and seasoned for his
passage" (*Hamlet*, III. iii. 86).

21. *honesty*] honourable character.
28. *his great right*] his fully justified
right, due to him as a great man.
34. *fistula*] a swelling on the breast,
aggravated by neglect. "Used in a
way as a sore." *Guard. Health,* 1579
(*New Eng. Dict.*).
39. *hopes*] expectations. Cf. "I
shall falsify men's hopes" (*1 Henry
IV.* I. ii. 235).
40. *her dispositions*] she derives her
honesty, without which no goodness
acquired by education could be fair.
I am inclined to think the reading

inherits, which makes fair gifts fairer; for where an unclean mind carries virtuous qualities, there commendations go with pity; they are virtues and traitors too: in her they are the better for their simpleness; she derives her honesty and 45 achieves her goodness.

Laf. Your commendations, madam, get from her tears.

Count. 'Tis the best brine a maiden can season her praise in. The remembrance of her father never 50 approaches her heart but the tyranny of her sorrows takes all livelihood from her cheek. No

45. *their*] *her* Hanmer (Warburton).

"disposition," is right, though the interpolation of "s" in the comedies is not frequent. Walker conjectures that this common misprint was due to some peculiarity in Shakespeare's handwriting which increased as he grew older. If so there seems to be no reason why this should not be one of these misprints—the passage being in all probability of later date than some of the rhymed portions.

42. *virtuous qualities*] This use of virtuous is akin to the Italian use of the word *virtuoso*, implying the *passione delle belle arti* made perfect by practice. Shakespeare is alluding only to those qualities which *can* be *acquired* by a mind either naturally honest or naturally unclean. In the north the word often meant "ingenious." Steevens understands it so here; as in Chapman's *Iliad*, viii. "our virtuous engine," and also Marlowe's *Tamburlaine*, Dyce, pt. i. v. ii. p. 33a:

"One thought, one grace, one wonder at the least,
Which into words no vertue can digest."

43. *go with pity*] go with regret, "pity" being often used to express what we call "a pity."

43, 44. *virtues and traitors*] Johnson has a long note on this expression, the meaning of which seems to be that cleverness (virtue) in an unclean mind is treacherous virtue (quality) because it inspires an admiration in others which tends to make them forget that it is "a pity."

45. *simpleness*] opposite of subtleness. Cf. R. Greene, *A Quip for an Upstart Courtier*, p. 1, "there grew many *simples* whose virtues taught me to be *subtle.*" There is an evident play on the words here.

48. *tears*] probably placed at the end of the sentence for emphasis and to "give the cue" to the following speech.

49. *season*] frequently used by Shakespeare. "Salt water (*i.e.* tears) to season love" (*Romeo and Juliet*, II. iii. 72). See also *Troilus and Cressida*, I. ii. 278; *Twelfth Night*, I. i. 30. It has been called a coarse metaphor; but, as Knight points out, it was in Jesus' mind when he said, "Ye are the salt of the earth" (Matt. v. 13). Cf. also L'Estrange's *Fables*: "children should be seasoned betimes and lessoned."

52. *livelihood*] animation (Middle English live-lode=life leading). This is the only use of the word in Shakespeare.

SC. I.]   THAT ENDS WELL   7

    more of this, Helena; go to, no more; lest it be
    rather thought you affect a sorrow than to have—
Hel. I do affect a sorrow indeed, but I have it too.   55
Laf. Moderate lamentation is the right of the dead,
    excessive grief the enemy to the living.
Count. If the living be enemy to the grief, the excess
    makes it soon mortal.
Ber. Madam, I desire your holy wishes.   60
Laf. How understand we that?

53, 54. *lest . . . have—*] *lest you be rather thought to* Hanmer, *. . . to have it.* Warburton, *to have.* Steevens, *have it.* Capell.   58. *If the living . . . grief*] *the grief be enemy to the living* Gould conj., *be not the enemy* Theobald (Warburton).   60, 61.] Theobald conj. transposes these two lines.

53. *lest . . .*] a strange construction, but the meaning is obvious:—lest you be thought rather to affect a sorrow than to feel it. Such slight inaccuracies are not peculiar to Shakespeare, as Malone has thought necessary to prove in detail.

54. *than to have—*] I think this must be left; it is impossible to say that Shakespeare did *not* write this: therefore we dare not change it.

55. *I do affect . . .*] Helena seems to be speaking half to herself—"there is indeed an outward show of sorrow, but I am really unhappy too." Cowden Clarke pertinently calls attention to the fact that these, Helena's first words, render her meaning so indistinctly that it is undivined by those around her, only half perceived even by the reader. It is the beginning of what the king calls "the bitter" (v. iii.), and the subject of the play is how the "bitter passed" and ended well.

58. *If the living . . .*] Johnson paraphrases, "If the living do not indulge grief, grief destroys itself by its own excess." Malone quotes *Winter's Tale*, v. iii. 51, in support of Johnson's interpretation:

    "... scarce any joy
Did ever live so long; no sorrow
But kill'd itself much sooner."

Also *Romeo and Juliet*, II. vi. 9: "These violent delights have violent ends, And in their triumph die." The word "mortal" often means "deadly" in Shakespeare. Cf. *Othello*, II. i. 72.—This whole speech has been assigned by many editors to Helena, and the arguments in favour of the suggestion are plausible. The great objection is that there seems to be little reason for doubting the correctness of the Ff. It is clearly an antithetical reply to Lafeu's remark, and logically belongs to the Countess, who said "no more of this" just before. Mr. Thiselton suggests that "the living"=the Countess; meaning "that if she did not combat Helena's grief, it would soon be the death of Helena."

61. *How . . . that?*] This is a strange speech. But it seems still stranger if we transpose it. Where place it? After line 55? then we have two speeches running. After 59? then Bertram's interruption is rude. Perhaps so. I cannot accept as unreservedly as does Mr. Thiselton Kinnear's "admirable" explanation that this is the "humourous allusion to the possibility of the Countess' wishes being anything else but holy."

Count. Be thou blest, Bertram; and succeed thy father
In manners, as in shape! thy blood and virtue
Contend for empire in thee; and thy goodness
Share with thy birthright! Love all, trust a few, 65
Do wrong to none: be able for thine enemy
Rather in power than use, and keep thy friend
Under thy own life's key: be check'd for silence,
But never tax'd for speech. What heaven more will
That thee may furnish, and my prayers pluck down, 70
Fall on thy head! [*To Lafeu*] Farewell, my lord;
'Tis an unseason'd courtier; good my lord,
Advise him.

68, 69. *check'd . . . tax'd*] *tax'd . . . check'd* Daniel conj. 71. *head* /]
F 1; *hand* F 2, 3, 4; *Farewell, my lord*] *Farewell my Lord* Ff, *Farewell—my lord Lafeu* Capell. 71-75.] Hanmer makes the lines end with *'tis an: advise him: attend: Bertram.* He is followed by Dyce. S. Walker gives lines ending with *my lord Lafeu: my lord: that shall: Bertram*, reading in line 74 *can't* for *cannot*. 73. *Advise him*] *advise him you* Capell.

65. *Share with*] be equal to. Cf. "Think not to share with me in glory any more" (*1 Henry IV.* v. iv. 64). With the following lines cf. Euphues's Advice to Philautus (The Complete Works of Lyly, ed. Warwick Bond, vol. ii. p. 223, etc.).

66. *be able*] Have power to daunt your foe, but practise not your power upon him. Cf. "Be ye angry and sin not." Johnson informs us that "able for" is not often nor very properly used. It occurs in Wilkins's *Mathematical Magic*, "There have been inventions which have been able for the utterance of articulate sounds." Cotgrave gives, "To be able or sufficient = être suffisant."

68. *check'd*] rebuked for being silent. Cf. *Julius Cæsar*, IV. iii. 97, "Check'd like a bondman." See also *2 Henry IV.* I. ii. 220.

69. *tax'd for*] blamed for. Cf. "he would not have taxed Milton for his choice of a supernatural argument." (Dryden.)

70. *That . . . furnish*] "When the unclean spirit is gone out of a man, he walketh through dry places, seeking rest; and finding none, he saith, I will return unto my house, whence I came out. And when he cometh, he findeth it swept and garnished." In the same way Shakespeare speaks of the spirit or mind being furnished. As in *Lear* (III. i. 29) furnishings mean appendages (that are not essential). The Countess prays for any superfluous gift that heaven may be willing to confer to embellish Bertram's character. In the same line "pluck" may be taken in its strong sense: "a team of horse shall not pluck that from me" (*Two Gentlemen of Verona*, III. i. 266). Or in its milder sense: "pluck a dainty doe to ground" (*Titus Andronicus*, II. ii. 26). The former seems more forceful in this passage.

72. *unseason'd*] See note, line 49, above.

Laf. He cannot want the best that shall attend
   His love.
Count.   Heaven bless him! Farewell, Bertram. 75
                                                  [*Exit.*
Ber. [*To Helena.*] The best wishes that can be forged
   in your thoughts be servants to you! Be com-
   fortable to my mother, your mistress, and make
   much of her.
Laf. Farewell, pretty lady: you must hold the credit 80
   of your father.   [*Exeunt Bertram and Lafeu.*
Hel. O! were that all. I think not on my father;
   And these great tears grace his remembrance more
   Than those I shed for him. What was he like?
   I have forgot him: my imagination   85

74. *the best*] Mr. Thiselton explains "the best *advice*," it being a compliment to the effect that he can have nothing to add to the excellent counsel the Countess has just given her son. The passage may be corrupt. Mr. Craig suggests "this lord" instead of "his love"—he who is a courtier in the service of this (feudal) lord cannot want the best. Mr. P. A. Daniel thinks that it is a case of punctuation—"He cannot want the best. That shall attend his love." The sense is not clear in the original, but the emendations are not quite convincing.

76. *The best wishes* . . .] Servants may here be used in the sense of lovers, as so frequently in the literature of chivalry. In that case the sentence would mean: May the best wishes you can frame for yourself fulfil your will as a lover would. Or else it is used in its straightforward sense as in *Coriolanus*, v. ii. 89, "my affairs are servanted to others." Mr. Thiselton takes this speech to be spoken by the Countess.

77, 78. *Be comfortable*] be full of comfort. Cf. "I have another daughter who, I am sure, is kind and comfortable." (*Lear*, I. iv. 327). Also "comfortable friar" (*Romeo and Juliet*, v. iii. 148), and the "comfortable words."

80. *hold*] Helena has said, "I have a sorrow," *i.e.* for the loss of my father, as Lafeu must have understood it. In parting he says, "You must hold the grief, hold the credit of your father." Some take it to mean "uphold." The passage is difficult, but it seems more reasonable to suppose that Helena was told to hold (cherish, remember) her father's credit, rather than to uphold it —a thing she could hardly do. And Helena's next exclamation, "O, were that all!" seems to indicate that she understands Lafeu's remark as referring to her feelings. "I *think not* on my father."

82. *O! were* . . .] Helena sees them all go, with kind words of sympathy for her fatherless condition; she cannot help exclaiming, "how small a part of all my woe is that!"

83, 84. *these . . . for him*] These tears grace Bertram's remembrance more than those I shed for my father. The meaning of the *his* is not obscure when accentuated by a gesture.

Carries no favour in 't but Bertram's.
I am undone: there is no living, none,
If Bertram be away. 'Twere all one
That I should love a bright particular star
And think to wed it, he is so above me: 90
In his bright radiance and collateral light
Must I be comforted, not in his sphere.
Th' ambition in my love thus plagues itself:
The hind that would be mated by the lion
Must die for love. 'Twas pretty, though a plague, 95
To see him every hour; to sit and draw
His arched brows, his hawking eye, his curls,
In our heart's table; heart too capable
Of every line and trick of his sweet favour:

88. *'Twere*] Ff, *It were* Pope and Dyce. 89. *particular*] *partic'lar* Pope. 90. *me*:] Rowe, *above me In* Ff. 96. *hour; to sit*] *hour to sit* Ff. 97. *brows*] *browes* F 1, 2; *arrows* F 3, 4. 98. *our*] *my* Collier (MS. notes).

86. *favour*] possibly a simile taken from the knight's custom of wearing his lady's favour or badge when fighting in a tourney. But perhaps the word merely means "face" as commonly.
91. *radiance* . . .] Steevens quotes Milton, *Paradise Lost*, x. 85, "from his radiant seat he rose Of high collateral glory." Cf. also *Hamlet*, IV. v. 206, "If by direct or by collateral hand they find us touch'd . . ." Here it means light emanating from a different sphere.
97. *hawking*] adjective, like the words charm-ing, middl-ing.
98. *table*] Malone explains this as "meaning 'picture,' French *tableau*." Boswell quotes the following in confirmation: "— he has a strange aspect, And looks much like the figure of a hangman In a table of the passion."
98. *capable*] ready to receive the impress of. See below, I. i. 215, "So thou wilt be capable of a courtier's counsel." The word capable refers to any kind of power or ability to *assume* a thing as in the sense of inheriting a thing. Cf. *Lear*, II. i. 87, "And of my land, loyal and natural boy, I'll work the means to make thee capable." See Mr. Craig's note on this passage in *Lear*. Also *Hamlet*, III. iv. 127.
99. *line and trick*] See *King John*, I. i. 85, "he hath a trick of Cœur de Lion's face." Line is often used by Shakespeare meaning "lineament." It is more especially the *out*line. See also *1 Henry IV*. v. ii. 11. In *Lear*, IV. vi. 108, we find "the trick of that voice." Trick means "characteristic" —something not in the "line." The Cambridge editors in their note on *King John*, I. i. 85, quote a note by Wilbraham. "*Trick* is a term in Heraldry for a *copy*." In the *Gentleman's Magazine* (1803, Sup. p. 1207), in an account of various memorandums of receipts and expenditures (etc.) by some one at the latter end of the seventeenth century,

But now he's gone, and my idolatrous fancy 100
Must sanctify his relics. Who comes here?

Enter PAROLLES.

[*Aside.*] One that goes with him: I love him for his
  sake;
And yet I know him a notorious liar,
Think him a great way fool, solely a coward;
Yet these fix'd evils sit so fit in him, 105
That they take place, when virtue's steely bones

102. Aside] Cambridge editors, omitted Ff.   106. *steely*] *seeley* Badham, *stately* Cartright conj.

are the following: "July 21st, 1691, Receiv'd of Mr. Cole for a trick of Consum's Arms, 2s. 6d.; July 25th, Mr. Martyn the Paynter for a trick of Lady Cath. Darnley's Arms, 2s. 6d.; Dec. 18th, Received of Mr. Gentry for a trick of Wyatt's Arms, 2s. 6d."

99. *favour*] countenance, as below, v. iii. 48, "Contempt . . . Which warp'd the line of every other favour."

101. *sanctify his relics*] relics or reliques = remembrance. See below, v. iii. 23, "The nature of his great offence is dead, And deeper than oblivion we do bury The *incensing relics* of it." Is this echo merely a chance one? Or is it one of the many instances of Shakespeare's irony—the image of nature's irony?

104. *a great way*] Cf. *Julius Cæsar*, II. i. 107, "Here the sun arises, which is a great way growing on the south, weighing the youthful season of the year."

104. *solely a coward*] entirely; a sheer coward. Boswell compares this use of "solely" with "only." Cf. *Cupid's Revenge*, "she being only wicked." Rolfe quotes *Macbeth*, I. v. 71, "Solely sovereign sway."

106. *take place*] are noticeable(?). Schmidt says, "are received as equals, in high society." Cowden Clarke gives "precedence" as the meaning. Mr. Thiselton's note is admirable: "evidently signifies more than it would at the present day. In *Utopia* we read, 'The whiche two vices of affection and avarice, where they take place in judgements' . . . (original Latin, *sicubi incubuere iudiciis*) . . . where Robinson, to judge by his usual practice, would have amplified, if 'take place' had not adequately represented the Latin. We may, therefore, conclude that 'take place' may mean 'take up their quarters.'"

106. *steely bones*] "steel-boned, unyielding, uncomplying virtue" (Schmidt). Steely is only used once elsewhere by Shakespeare: "the steely point of Clifford's lance" (*3 Henry VI.* II. iii. 16). Bones might here be a singular noun meaning body; in which case "lookes" of the Ff would be correct. Badham reads "seely bones." Does he understand a reference to "funny-bone," which was often called "crazy-bone," but not, so far as I am aware, "silly-bone"? It seems somewhat difficult to accept the explanation "when virtue's silly bones look bleak i' the cold wind," meaning "out at elbow."

Look bleak i' th cold wind: withal, full oft we see
Cold wisdom waiting on superfluous folly."
Par. Save you, fair queen!
Hel. And you, monarch! 110
Par. No.
Hel. And no.
Par. Are you meditating on virginity?
Hel. Ay. You have some stain of soldier in you;
let me ask you a question. Man is enemy to 115
virginity; how may we barricado it against him?
Par. Keep him out.
Hel. But he assails; and our virginity, though valiant,
in the defence yet is weak. Unfold to us some
warlike resistance. 120
Par. There is none: man, setting down before you,
will undermine you and blow you up.

107. *Look*] Rowe, *bones Lookes* Ff, *bone Looks* Bulloch conj.; *i' th*] Ff, *in the* Pope. Hudson suggests omitting "cold" and Pope "withal." Kinnear instead of "wind: withal" would write "wind without:". 108. *Cold*] S. Walker thinks that this word is corrupt (*Crit. Ex.* iii. 71), perhaps "poor." 117, 118. *Keep him out.* Hel. *But*] *Keep him out?* Hel. *For he* Hanmer. 118. *assails ;*] *assails us ;* S. Walker conj. (*Crit. Ex.* ii. 263). 121. *setting*] *sitting* Johnson.

107. *withal*] therewith.
108. *Cold . . . folly*] cold for naked; superfluous for overclothed (Warburton). Poor wisdom waiting on too rich folly. Dyce quotes, "our basest beggars are in the poorest things superfluous" (*Lear*, II. iv. 268). S. Walker would read "poor" instead of "cold," and take the first cold (cold wind) to be an interpolation: the whole passage to run, ". . . That they take place, when virtue's silly bone Looks bleak i' th' wind: withal, full oft we see Cold wisdom waiting on superfluous folly."
110. *monarch*] perhaps an allusion to that "vain fantastical man" called Monarcho (cf. Armado in *Love's Labour's Lost*).

114. *some stain*] "some qualities, at least superficial" (Johnson). Cf. *Troilus and Cressida*, I. ii. 26, "there is no man hath a virtue that he hath not a glimpse of, nor any man an attaint but he carries some stain of it."
121. *setting down*] laying siege. "All places yield to him ere he sets down" (*Coriolanus*, IV. vii. 28). Mr. Thiselton quotes the following passages from *Euphues*: "'And though women have small force to overcome men by reason, yet have they good fortune to undermine them by policie. The soft droppes of raine perce hard Marble, many strokes overthrow the tallest Oke, a silly woman in time may make such a breach into a man's heart, as hir

Hel. Bless our poor virginity from underminers and
blowers up! Is there no military policy, how
virgins might blow up men? 125
Par. Virginity being blown down, man will quicklier
be blown up: marry, in blowing him down
again, with the breach yourselves made, you lose
your city. It is not politic in the common-
wealth of nature to preserve virginity. Loss of 130
virginity is rational increase, and there was never
virgin got till virginity was first lost. That you
were made of is metal to make virgins. Virginity,
by being once lost, may be ten times found:
by being ever kept, it is ever lost. 'Tis too cold 135
a companion: away with 't!

131. *rational*] *national* Hanmer (Theobald conj.), *natural* Anon. conj. (*ap.* Halliwell). 132. *got*] F 2, *goe* F 1.

teares may enter without resistance'
—which seems to fix the meanings
of 'blowne downe.' 'Blowne up'
means made to spring into 'bloom,'
and also inflated with victory, and
in fact all possible meanings of 'blow
up' and 'blow down' are intended
in the course of the passage. Parolles'
remarks on virginity seem to have been
suggested by the conversation between
Ferardo and Lucilla in *Euphues*, from
which the following is extracted: 'But
this grieveth me most, that thou art
almost vowed to the vayne order of the
vestal virgins, dispising, or at least not
desiring the sacred bandes of Juno hir
bedde. If thy mother had bene of
that minde when she was a mayden,
thou haddest not nowe bene borne, to
be of this minde to be a virgin. Way
with thy selfe what slender profit they
bring to the common wealth, what
slight pleasure to themselves, what
great grief to their parents, which joy
most in their off-spring, and desire
most to enjoy the noble and blessed
name of a graundfather. Thou knowest
. . . that the woman that maketh hir
selfe barren by not marrying, is ac-
compted amonge the Grecian Ladyes
worse than a carryon, as Homer re-
porteth': and again, 'that honourable estate of Matrimony, which was
sanctified in Paradise, allowed of the
Patriarches, hallowed of the olde Pro-
phets, and commended of all persons'."
(ed. Bond, vol. i. p. 229, etc.).

129. *city*] a maid's innocence.
Malone quotes the *Lover's Complaint*:
" And long upon these terms I held
my city Till thus he 'gan besiege me."
And the *Rape of Lucrece*: " This
made in him more rage, and lesser
pity To make the breach and enter
this sweet city."

131. *rational*] reasonable. Cf.
Glanville's *Scepsis*: "When the conclusion is deduced from the unerring
dictates of our faculties, we say the
inference is rational."

Hel. I will stand for 't a little, though therefore I die a virgin.

Par. There's little can be said in 't; 'tis against the rule of nature. To speak on the part of virginity 140 is to accuse your mothers, which is most infallible disobedience. He that hangs himself is a virgin: virginity murders itself, and should be buried in highways out of all sanctified limit, as a desperate offendress against nature. Virginity 145 breeds mites, much like a cheese, consumes itself to the very paring, and so dies with feeding his own stomach. Besides, virginity is peevish, proud, idle, made of self-love, which is the most inhibited sin in the canon. Keep it not; you 150 cannot choose but lose by 't. Out with 't! within one year it will make itself two, which is

147. *paring*] Rowe; *payring* F 1, 2.   152. *one year . . . two*] Grant White and Dyce; *ten yeare (yeares or years) . . . two* Ff; *ten months . . . two* Singer; *the year . . . two* Anon. conj. and Delius; *ten year . . . ten* Cambridge editors and Globe edition; *two years . . . two* Collier, ed. 2 (Steevens conj.); *ten years . . . twelve* Tollet conj.

137. *stand for 't*] fight for 't. Shylock in the court of judgment says, "I stand for judgment . . . I stand for law." See also *Winter's Tale*, III. ii. 46, "For honour 'Tis a derivative from me to mine; And only that I stand for."

140. *on the part of*] side, party. "My father came on the part of York" (*3 Henry VI*, II. v. 66). "I'll fight against the part I come with" (*Cymbeline*, v. i. 25).

142. *He that hangs . . .*] he that commits suicide is like a virgin: both put an end to their own existence. (Malone.)

144. *sanctified limit*] Cf. Harrison, *Description of England*, II. chap. ii., "such as kill themselves are buried in the field with a stake through their bodies." (W. J. C.).

150. *inhibited*] forbidden. "a practiser of arts inhibited and out of warrant" (*Othello*, I. ii. 79).

150. *in the canon*] Cf. *Hamlet*, I. ii. 131, "O, that the Everlasting had not fixed His canon 'gainst self-slaughter."

151. *Out with 't*] not the same as "Keep it not." It implies giving or putting a thing out to interest. (Malone compares *Tempest*, III. iii. 48.) The idea is borne out by the subsequent words of Parolles.

152. *within . . . two*] The Ff have within ten . . . two. A famous crux. Sir Th. Hanmer's emendation has been adopted by the Cambridge editors and in

a goodly increase, and the principal itself not
much the worse. Away with 't!

Hel. How might one do, sir, to lose it to her own 155
liking?

Par. Let me see: marry, ill, to like him that ne'er it
likes. 'Tis a commodity will lose the gloss with
lying; the longer kept, the less worth: off with
't while 'tis vendible; answer the time of request. 160
Virginity, like an old courtier, wears her cap out
of fashion; richly suited, but unsuitable: just
like the brooch and the toothpick, which wear
not now. Your date is better in your pie and
your porridge than in your cheek: and your 165
virginity, your old virginity, is like one of our
French withered pears; it looks ill, it eats drily;
marry, 'tis a withered pear; it was formerly

157, 158. *it likes*] *likes it* S. Walker conj. (*Crit. Ex.* ii. 248).   163. *wear*] Capell, *were* Ff, *we wear* Rowe.

the Globe edition; Malone's arguments in favour of this reading are forcible. But if the editors of the later folios changed the "yeare" of the first Folio because of the "*ten* yeare," editors who give "ten years" accept the emendation of the later folios, which is at least disputable. To suppose, as Grant White does, that the 1623 folio printed "ten" by mistake instead of "one" is certainly the simplest and perhaps the safest way of taking this much discussed passage.

157. *to like* . . .] to love the man who puts an end to virginity.

157, 158. *it likes*] in all probability "it" is accusative governed by "likes," *i.e.* that ne'er likes it. S, Walker would change the text to "likes it."

159. *lying*] as in *Taming of the Shrew*, II. 330, "'Twas a commodity lay fretting by you."

163. *toothpick*] probably first used in Italy, and at one time only used in England by those who affected foreign customs. Cf. "your traveller, he and his toothpick at my worship's mess" (*John*, I. i. 190).

163, 164. *wear not now*] are not the fashion. Cf. "Motley's the only wear" (*As You Like It*, II. vii. 34). "Any toys for your head of the newest and finest wear" (*Winter's Tale*, IV. iv. 327).

164. *date*] There is a pun here on the two meanings of date (a fruit, time of life), not quite clear, because dates are no longer "the candied fruit much used" for pastry and other dishes. Cf. *Troilus and Cressida*, I. ii. 280, "And then to be bak'd with no date in the pie, for then the man's date is out." (Steevens.)

better; marry, yet 'tis a withered pear. Will
you any thing with it? 170
Hel. Not my virginity yet. . . .
There shall your master have a thousand loves,
A mother, and a mistress, and a friend,
A phœnix, captain, and an enemy,

169. *yet*] *yes* Hanmer. 170. *with it?*] *with me?* Johnson conj.; *with us?* Tyrwhitt conj.; *with it? We are for the Court* Staunton conj. 171. *Not . . . yet*] *No!—my virginity! yet There shall its* Jackson conj.; Hanmer suggests "*yet. You're for the court.*"

169. *yet'tis*] Hanmer suggests "yes," which is quite a likely reading. Cf. *Cymbeline*, "Faith, yes." But probably "yet" is here used meaning "now." He has just said, "it was formerly better; marry, *now* 'tis a withered pear." The word "yet" is frequently used in this sense (cf. *Coriolanus*, IV. iii. 5, IV. v. 69, etc.).

169, 170. *Will you any thing with it?*] A common expression in the sixteenth century, conveying no particular signification beyond a certain saucy flippancy, like our modern "if you wish to know," "so now you know." Cf. Hale's *Criminal Cases* cited by Mr. Froude in his *History of England* (i. p. 181, ed. 1): "The apparitor of the Bishop of London went with a citation into the shop of a mercer . . . 'Who does cite me?' asked the mercer. 'Marry, that do I,' answered the apparitor, 'if thou wilt anything with it'—Whereupon . . . (the said mercer) did, snatch up his virga—Anglice, his yard—and did pursue the apparitor into the public streets, and, after multiplying of many blows, did break the head of the said apparitor." (Dyce.)

171. *Not . . . yet . . .*] Something must have been lost here, perhaps several lines. I sympathise with Johnson, who said, "I know not what to do with the passage." If the abrupt stop at "yet" is not due to the omission of something, there might conceivably have been a mistake about the parts: the Page may have entered in the middle of Helena's sentence. But that means recasting the whole passage, which is quite impossible. The next few lines may be looked upon as an example of dramatic prophecy—by means of which the subject is constantly kept before us. Cf. lower down, I. ii. 72, where the King says, "If he were living, I would try him," suggesting to *us* that he will try the daughter.

173. *mother*] Dr. Herford suggests that "this word is perhaps the same as 'mauther,' an old provincial word for a young girl or maid . . . Cf. Ben Jonson's *Alchemist*, ed. H. C. Hart, IV. 4, 641. 'Away! You talk like a foolish mauther.' It was sometimes written modder . . . and, as Brome has it, with an evident quibble, 'Where maids are mothers, and mothers are maids.'" According to Nares the word is still used in Norfolk and Suffolk. Doubtful in this passage.

174. *captain*] All these terms are often used as epithets of endearment. Cf. *Winter's Tale*, I. ii. 122, where Leontes says to young Mamillius, "Come, captain, we must be neat . . ."; and in the same scene Polixenes, speaking of his son, says, "He's all my exercise, my mirth, my matter; Now my sworn friend, and then mine enemy; My parasite, my soldier, statesman, all." (Malone.) Steevens's note is to the point: "Our ancient writers delighted in catalogues, and always characterised love by contrarieties."

A guide, a goddess, and a sovereign,   175
A counsellor, a traitress, and a dear;
His humble ambition, proud humility,
His jarring, concord, and his discord, dulcet,
His faith, his sweet disaster; with a world
Of pretty fond-adoptious christendoms,   180
That blinking Cupid gossips. Now shall he—
I know not what he shall. God send him well!
The court's a learning-place, and he is one—
Par. What one, i' faith?
Hel. That I wish well. 'Tis pity—   185
Par. What's pity?
Hel. That wishing well had not a body in't,
Which might be felt; that we, the poorer born,
Whose baser stars do shut us up in wishes,
Might with effects of them follow our friends,   190

---

179. *His faith, his*] *His faithless* Hanmer.   180. *fond-adoptious*] S. Walker conj. (adopted by Dyce), *pretty fond adoptious* Ff.

179. *faith, his sweet*] Hanmer conjectured 'faith less sweet.' But how can we change a passage that is meant to be nonsense?

180. *fond-adoptious christendoms*] adopted names of love. This use of the word christendom to signify "christian name" seems rare. Malone quotes an instance from Nash in *Four Letters Confuted*: "But for an author to renounce his christendom to write in his owne commendation, to refuse the name his godfather and godmothers gave him in baptism. . . ." No other instance of the word "adoptious" is known.

181. *gossips*] verb, used in the old sense of acting as sponsor. The change of meaning had perhaps already begun in Shakespeare's time, for we find him using the word with reference to the women who waited on mothers during childbirth. It is Cupid who gives these "fond-adoptious christendoms."

189. *baser stars*] base as belonging to the poorer born=the base. "Our basest beggars are in the poorest things superfluous" (*Lear*, II. iv. 267). "And base things of the world and things which are despised hath God chosen" (1 Cor. i. 28).

190. *with*] with the, wi' th'. (Herford.)

190. *with effects*] An effect is the result or fulfilment of a wish or purpose. "Do not look upon me, Lest with this piteous action you convert My stern effects" (*Hamlet*, III. iv. 129). "Thoughts are but dreams till their effects be tried" (*Lucrece*, 353). "Our wishes may prove effects" (*Lear*, IV. ii. 15).

And show what we alone must think, which never
Returns us thanks.

Enter a Page.

Page. Monsieur Parolles, my lord calls for you.   [*Exit.*
Par. Little Helen, farewell: if I can remember thee,
I will think of thee at court.   195
Hel. Monsieur Parolles, you were born under a
charitable star.
Par. Under Mars, I.
Hel. I especially think, under Mars.
Par. Why under Mars?   200
Hel. The wars have so kept you under, that you must
needs be born under Mars.
Par. When he was predominant.
Hel. When he was retrograde, I think rather.
Par. Why think you so?   205
Hel. You go so much backward when you fight.
Par. That's for advantage.
Hel. So is running away, when fear proposes the
safety: but the composition that your valour
and fear makes in you is a virtue of a good wing, 210
and I like the wear well.
Par. I am so full of businesses, I cannot answer thee
acutely. I will return perfect courtier; in the

201. *wars have*] Pope; *warres hath* F 1, 2; *waters halth* F 3, 4; *waters have* Rowe.   211. *I like the*] *is like to* Mason conj.   212. *businesses*] *business* F 4.

191. *show*] as in the phrases, show pity, show justice.
191. *alone must think*] must only think.
209. *composition*] cf. IV. iii. 18, below.
211. *I like the wear*] Mason suggests "and is like to wear well." See note on line 163.

which my instruction shall serve to naturalize
thee, so thou wilt be capable of a courtier's 215
counsel, and understand what advice shall thrust
upon thee; else thou diest in thine unthankful-
ness, and thine ignorance makes thee away:
farewell. When thou hast leisure, say thy
prayers; when thou hast none, remember thy 220
friends. Get thee a good husband, and use him
as he uses thee: so farewell. [*Exit.*

Hel. Our remedies oft in ourselves do lie
Which we ascribe to heaven: the fated sky
Gives us free scope; only doth backward pull 225
Our slow designs when we ourselves are dull.
What power is it which mounts my love so high,
That makes me see, and cannot feed mine eye?
The mightiest space in fortune nature brings
To join like likes, and kiss like native things. 230

220. *none,*] *money,* Williams conj.   229. *The mightiest space*] *The wid'st apart* Staunton conj., *through mightiest space* Johnson; *fortune nature*] *nature fortune* Rann (Malone conj.); *brings*] *springs* Anon. conj. (*Fras. Mag.*, 1853). 230. *To join like likes*] *Likes to join likes* Johnson conj., *Like to join like* Long MS.

214. *naturalize*] teach. Cf. South, "He rises fresh to his hammer and anvil; custom has naturalized his labour to him."
215. *capable of*] See article on line 98, above.
218. *makes thee away*] makes away with thee. "So in thyself thyself art made away" (*Venus and Adonis*, 763). "Three score year would make the world away" (*Sonnets*, xi. 8).
220. *none*] no leisure? absolute nonsense. Perhaps Parolles is meant to be talking nonsense. If not, Williams's conjecture that "none" is a misprint for "money" is almost certainly right.
224. *fated*] fateful. Cf. "The plagues hang fated o'er men's faults" (*Lear,* III. iv.).
227. *high*] Bertram's rank high as compared with hers.
229, 230. *brings To join*] succeed in making. "I cannot bring my tongue to such a pace" (*Coriolanus*, II. iii. 56). Malone paraphrases, "The affections given us by nature often unite persons between whom fortune or accident has placed the greatest distance or disparity, and causes them to join, like likes (*instar parium*) like persons in the same situation or rank of life." Mr. Thiselton quotes: "So that I fear they do but bring Extreams to touch, and mean one thing" (Jonson's *The Sad Shepherd*, I. v.).

Impossible be strange attempts to those
That weigh their pains in sense, and do suppose
What hath been cannot be. Who ever strove
To show her merit that did miss her love?
The king's disease—my project may deceive me, 235
But my intents are fix'd and will not leave me. [*Exit.*

SCENE II.—*Paris. A Room in the King's Palace.*

Flourish of cornets. Enter the KING, *with letters; Lords and others attending.*

King. The Florentines and Senoys are by th' ears;
Have fought with equal fortune, and continue
A braving war.

233. *What . . . be*] *hath not been can't be* Hanmer, *ha'nt been cannot be* Mason conj., *n'ath been cannot be* Staunton conj., *hath been can but be* Bulloch conj. Perhaps, "What hath not, cannot, be."

The anonymous conjecture in the *Fras. Mag.*, 1853, substituting "springs" for "brings" is good. But it is not a suggestion to adopt.

231. *Impossible*] inconceivable. "And what impossibility would slay In common sense, sense saves another way" (II. i. 178, below). Here again Mr. Thiselton very aptly quotes from *Euphues*: "Neither am I so wedded to the world that I should be moved with great possessions, neither so bewitched with wantonnesse, that I should be entysed with any mans proportion, neither if I were so disposed would I be so proude, to desire one of noble proginie, or so precise to choose one onely of mine owne countrey, for that commonly these things happen alwayes to the contrary. Doe we not see the noble to match with the base, the rich with the poore, the Italian oftentimes with the Portingale? As love knoweth no lawes, so it regardeth no conditions; and as the lover maketh no pawse where he lyketh, so he maketh no conscience of these idle ceremonies."

233. *hath been*] One is tempted to adopt Hanmer's suggestion, "ha'n't been." There is, as editors have not been slow to point out, plenty of sense to be wrung out of "what hath been cannot be." But it is so unusual a phrase, whereas "what ha'n't been cannot be" is what one would expect.

Scene II.

1. *Senoys*] natives of Siena, distant from Florence about thirty miles. Paynter spells the word "Senois." Boccaccio calls them "Sanesi."

1. *by th' ears*] quarrel. "Were half to half the world by th' ears . . ." (*Coriolanus*, I. i. 237). The metaphor is taken from fighting animals and in old writers the commonest form is "go together by the ears" (W. J. C.).

3. *braving*] Cf. "in braving arms against thy sovereign" (*Richard II.* II. iii. 112).

First Lord.   So 'tis reported, sir.
King. Nay, 'tis most credible: we here receive it
    A certainty, vouch'd from our cousin Austria,   5
    With caution, that the Florentine will move us
    For speedy aid; wherein our dearest friend
    Prejudicates the business, and would seem
    To have us make denial.
First Lord.   His love and wisdom,
    Approv'd so to your majesty, may plead   10
    For amplest credence.
King.   He hath arm'd our answer,
    And Florence is denied before he comes:
    Yet, for our gentlemen that mean to see
    The Tuscan service, freely have they leave
    To stand on either part.
Second Lord.   It well may serve   15
    A nursery to our gentry, who are sick
    For breathing and exploit.
King.   What's he comes here?

        Enter BERTRAM, LAFEU, *and* PAROLLES.
First Lord. It is the Count Rousillon, my good lord,
    Young Bertram.

  18. *Count Rousillon*] Pope, *Count Rosignoll* F 1.

  4. *credible*] the first lord has just
qualified the King's statement by saying, "So 'tis reported," and the King
answers, "it is credible," *i.e. certainly*
trustworthy, reliable.
  5. *cousin*] a title among princes.
Mr. Craig tells me that in the North of
Ireland they say of an arrogant person,
"he would not call the King his
cousin."
  6. *move us*] ask us.

  10. *Approv'd so*] proved, made evident by proof. See below, line 50, "So
in approof lives not his epitaph As in
your royal speech."
  16. *nursery*] original meaning, a
place for satisfying hunger.
  17. *breathing*] activity. See below,
II. iii. 259, "I think thou wast
created for men to breathe themselves
upon thee." We say, "let off steam."

King.   Youth, thou bear'st thy father's face;
          Frank nature, rather curious than in haste,   20
          Hath well compos'd thee. Thy father's moral
             parts
          May'st thou inherit too! Welcome to Paris.
Ber. My thanks and duty are your majesty's.
King. I would I had that corporal soundness now,
          As when thy father and myself in friendship   25
          First tried our soldiership! He did look far
          Into the service of the time, and was
          Discipled of the bravest: he lasted long;
          But on us both did haggish age steal on,
          And wore us out of act. It much repairs me   30
          To talk of your good father. In his youth
          He had the wit, which I can well observe
          To-day in our young lords; but they may jest
          Till their own scorn return to them unnoted

21. *well compos'd thee*] *compos'd thee well* Pope.

20. *curious*] Mr. Craig in his note on the word "curiosity" (*Lear,* I. i. 6, etc.) gives "a man must not go too hastily to it (shooting with the bow), for that is rashness, nor yet make too much to do about it, for that is curiosity." (Ascham, *Toxophilus,* Arber, p. 147), ". . . Who overthrew himself in his doings, not so much for lack of reasonable skill of Warres, as through his unprofitable curiositie and strictness in observing the law." The word curious occurs in Ex. xxviii. 8, "The curious (=embroidered) girdle of the ephod." Ps. cxxxix., "I was made in secret, and curiously wrought."

21. *Hath*] This word is suspiciously like an interpolation — the repetition of the word "haste" at the end of the preceding line.

26. *He did look far*] was a man who had seen much active service.

28. *discipled of*] taught by.

30. *act*] activity or power to take part in action.

33. *they may jest*] "your father (says the King) had the same airy flights of satirical wit with the young lords of the present time, but they do not what he did, hide their unnoted levity in honour, cover petty faults with great merit." Johnson, whose paraphrase this is, considers it "an excellent observation. Jocose follies, and slight offences, are only allowed by mankind in him that overpowers them by great qualities." There is an old saying: "young men are subtle arguers: the cloak of honour covers all their faults, as that of passion all their follies."

Ere they can hide their levity in honour. 35
So like a courtier, contempt nor bitterness
Were in his pride or sharpness; if they were,
His equal had awak'd them; and his honour,
Clock to itself, knew the true minute when
Exception bid him speak, and at this time 40
His tongue obey'd his hand: who were below him
He us'd as creatures of another place,
And bow'd his eminent top to their low ranks,
Making them proud of his humility,
In their poor praise he humbled. Such a man 45
Might be a copy to these younger times,
Which, followed well, would demonstrate them now
But goers backward.

Ber. His good remembrance, sir,

35. *in honour*] *in humour* Long MS. (and independently Dyce conj.). 35, 36. *honour. So . . . courtier*] *honour: So like a courtier* Ff. 42. *of another place*] *of a brother race* Hanmer, *of a nobler place* Williams conj. 44. *proud of*] *proud ; and* Warburton (Williams conj.). 45. *In . . . humbled*] *be-humbled* Staunton conj., *He, in . . . praise, humbled* Becket conj., *praise the humbler* Williams conj. (reading line 44 with Warburton); perhaps *so humbled*.

35. *in honour*] Long MS. and Dyce read "humour." I see no reason.
36. *So like a courtier*] Sir William Blackstone suggested placing a stop after "courtier," and was followed by Capell, Rolfe, and others. Johnson, accepting no emendation, paraphrases "He was so like a courtier that there was in his dignity of manner nothing contemptuous, and in his keenness of wit nothing bitter. If bitterness or contemptuousness ever appeared, they had been awakened by some injury, not of a man below him, but of his equal."
39. *true*] proper. Cf. "truepenny," and below, II. v. 6, "my dial goes not true."
40. *Exception*] disapproval. The same word is used in *Hamlet*, V. ii. 241,
"What I have done That might your nature, honour and exception Roughly awake."
41. *his hand*] the clock's hand.
42. *of another place*] perhaps "strangers, men to whom it was necessary to be courteous." The passage is obscure. "Another place" is strange; Williams's conjecture "nobler place" seems better, but hardly right. Perhaps "an other place" means "an equal place" in the sense of "second and equal," as when "other" is used with "the." Perhaps instead of "he humbled" we might read "so humbled." Malone explains the construction as being equivalent to "he being humbled in their poor praise." Williams tries to escape the difficulty by reading "in their poor praise *the* humbler."

Lies richer in your thoughts than on his tomb;
So in approof lives not his epitaph   50
As in your royal speech.
King. Would I were with him! He would always say,—
Methinks I hear him now: his plausive words
He scatter'd not in ears, but grafted them,
To grow there and to bear;—" Let me not live,"— 55
Thus his good melancholy oft began,
On the catastrophe and heel of pastime,
When it was out,—" Let me not live," quoth he,
" After my flame lacks oil, to be the snuff
Of younger spirits, whose apprehensive senses   60
All but new things disdain; whose judgments are

56. *Thus*] Pope, *This* Ff.   58. *it*] *wit* Staunton conj.; *was*] *wears* Kinnear conj. (putting line 56 in a parenthesis).

50. *So in approof*] "His epitaph lives far better in your royal speech than it could in the remembrance of posterity." Approvers were men who tried the accused; and the verb "approve" is used in the sense of increasing or supporting a reputation: as in "if you did, it would not much approve me" (*Hamlet*, V. ii. 141) (Dyce). Bertram means that the King's words give life to the epitaph which as a rule can only live in the judgment (approof) of posterity. Cf. "of very valiant approof" (II. v. 3, below). "And as my farthest band shall pass on thy approof" (*Antony and Cleopatra*, III. ii. 27).

53. *plausive*] pleasing; as in *Hamlet*, I. iv. 30, "his plausive manners."

54. *scatter'd not in ears*] Knight quotes: "Grant, we beseech Thee, . . . that the words which we have heard with our outward ears may . . . be so grafted inwardly in our hearts, that they may bring forth the fruit of good living." [The Book of Common Prayer. *The Communion.*]

57. *catastrophe . . . heel*] both words mean "end." "When April on the heel of limping winter treads" (*Romeo and Juliet*, I. ii. 27).

58. *out*] Staunton conjectured "wit," evidently unable to get any meaning out of the passage as it stands. Most editors have, I believe, taken the "it" to refer to "pastime"—"when the pastime was over." It might also refer to "melancholy"—and the "was out" would then mean being at a loss for something to say (down in the mouth). "Thus his good melancholy oft began . . . when it was out (of sorts)." Cf. *Love's Labour's Lost*, V. ii. 152, 165, 172; *As You Like It*, IV. i. 76, 82; *Coriolanus*, V. iii. 41.

59. *snuff*] Cf. Mal. i. 13, "Ye have snuffed at (my table), saith the Lord." The margin gives "whereas ye might have blown it away." Cf. also "Left, like an unsavoury snuff . . . Whose property is only to offend" (Jonson's *Every Man in his Humour*).

60. *apprehensive*] Falstaff says, "a good sherris-sack . . . makes the brain apprehensive, quick, forgetive (inventive)" (*2 Henry* IV. iii. 107). Shakespeare uses it several times in this sense.

   Mere fathers of their garments; whose constancies
   Expire before their fashions." This he wish'd:
   I, after him, do after him wish too,
   Since I nor wax nor honey can bring home,   65
   I quickly were dissolved from my hive,
   To give some labourers room.
Second Lord.   You are lov'd, sir;
   They that least lend it you shall lack you first.
King. I fill a place; I know 't. How long is 't, count,
   Since the physician at your father's died?   70
   He was much fam'd.
Ber.   Some six months since, my lord.
King. If he were living, I would try him yet.
   Lend me an arm: the rest have worn me out
   With several applications: nature and sickness
   Debate it at their leisure. Welcome, count;   75
   My son's no dearer.
Ber.   Thank your majesty.
             [*Flourish. Exeunt.*

   SCENE III.—*Rousillon. A Room in the*
       Countess's Palace.

   Enter COUNTESS, *Steward, and Clown.*

Count. I will now hear: what say you of this gentlewoman?

---

62. *fathers*] *feathers* Tyrwhitt conj., *parcels* Williams conj.   67. *You are*] Capell, *you'r* or *you're* Ff.

62. *fathers of their garments*] their judgments did nothing but give birth to new designs for clothes. Cf. "Every minute now Should be the father of some stratagem" (Malone). Also, "Thy wish was father to that thought" (*2 Henry IV.* IV. v. 93).
66. *dissolved*] discharged. Cf. *Merry Wives*, V. v. 237.

Stew. Madam, the care I have had to even your
content, I wish might be found in the calendar
of my past endeavours; for then we wound our   5
modesty and make foul the clearness of our
deservings, when of ourselves we publish them.
Count. What does this knave here? Get you gone,
sirrah; the complaints I have heard of you I do
not all believe: 'tis my slowness that I do not;   10
for I know you lack not folly to commit them, and
have ability enough to make such knaveries yours.
Clo. 'Tis not unknown to you, madam, I am a poor
fellow.
Count. Well, sir.   15
Clo. No, madam, 'tis not so well that I am poor,
though many of the rich are damned. But, if I
may have your ladyship's good will to go to the
world, Isbel your woman and I will do as we may.
Count. Wilt thou needs be a beggar?   20

18. *to go to*] *to go* F 3, 4.   19. *your*] Badham, *the* Ff; *and I will*] F 2, 3, 4; *and w will* F 1; *and we will* Collier.

3. *even*] the transitive verb "even" is only twice used by Shakespeare. "But we'll even all that good time will give us" (*Cymbeline*, III. iv. 184). It is borrowed from the language of accountants, as Mr. Craig points out in his note on *to make even* in *Lear*, IV. vii. 80. Cotgrave has "egaler=to equall, even, levell, match." The meaning here is that the steward has had a care to make his endeavours balance with, or even her wishes.

4. *calendar*] record (*New Eng. Dict.*). Bacon writes: "Shepherds of people had best know the calendars of tempests of state."

8. *What . . . here?*] The Steward beats about the bush, because he has the delicacy to shrink from making known his discovery to the Countess in the presence of a third party—and such a third party too! The word "publish" is a strong hint to her to dismiss the clown, which she promptly takes. The clown, however, makes the most of his privileges, and airs his wit before he goes. (A. E. Thiselton.)

11. *commit them*] a curious construction: but the meaning is clear.

18, 19. *go to the world*] be married. Cf. *As You Like It*, V. iii. 5. "Thus goes every one to the world but I" (*Much Ado*, II. i. 330).

19. *do as we may*] as best we can. Cf. Fitzherbert on Husbandry: after saying that a cowe gives more milk

Clo. I do beg your good will in this case.
Count. In what case?
Clo. In Isbel's case and mine own. Service is no
    heritage; and I think I shall never have the
    blessing of God till I have issue o' my body, for   25
    they say barnes are blessings.
Count. Tell me thy reason why thou wilt marry.
Clo. My poor body, madam, requires it: I am driven
    on by the flesh; and he must needs go that the
    devil drives.   30
Count. Is this all your worship's reason?
Clo. Faith, madam, I have other holy reasons, such
    as they are.
Count. May the world know them?
Clo. I have been, madam, a wicked creature, as you   35
    and all flesh and blood are; and indeed, I do
    marry that I may repent.
Count. Thy marriage, sooner than thy wickedness.
Clo. I am out o' friends, madam; and I hope to
    have friends for my wife's sake.   40
Count. Such friends are thine enemies, knave.

25. *o' my body*] Rowe (ed. 2), *a my body* Ff.   39. *out o'*] Capell; *out a* F 1, 2, 3; *out of* F 4.

when fed on grasse than on heye, he goes on, "But he that hath no pasture, must do as he may" (Skeat, 1882, p. 58). W. J. C.

23. *Service ... .*] a proverb. Gollancz says, "the idea seems to be that if service is no blessing, children are." Mr. Craig pointed out to me a passage in the *History of George a Greene Pickering* (ed. 1827, p. 9), "he remembered himself of the . . . English proverb 'that service is no hermitage'." (*sic*). We may take it that he was trying to "remember himself" of our proverb.

26. *barnes*] old form of the word for children now spelled "bairns" in Scotland. Occurs several times in Shakespeare.

29, 30. *he must ... drives*] proverbial.

32. *holy reasons*] reasons connected with religion. "Holy vows" occurs in *A Lover's Complaint*, 179.

Clo. You're shallow, madam; e'en great friends; for
the knaves come to do that for me which I am
aweary of. He that ears my land spares my team,
and gives me leave to in the crop: if I be his   45
cuckold, he's my drudge. He that comforts my
wife is the cherisher of my flesh and blood; he
that cherishes my flesh and blood loves my flesh
and blood; he that loves my flesh and blood is
my friend: *ergo,* he that kisses my wife is my   50
friend. If men could be contented to be what
they are, there were no fear in marriage; for
young Charbon the puritan, and old Poysam the
papist, howsomere their hearts are severed in
religion, their heads are both one; they may jowl   55
horns together, like any deer i' the herd.

Count. Wilt thou ever be a foul-mouthed and calum-
nious knave?

42. *You're*] Capell, *y'are* Ff; *e'en*] Hanmer, *in* Ff.   53. *Charbon . . .
Poysam*] see article below.   54. *howsomere*] F 4; *how somere* F 1, 2; *how-
someere* F 3; *howsoe'er* Pope.

42. *e'en*] Malone adopted this change, thinking that "*in* great friends" was evidently a way of writing "e'en." The same spelling occurs in many other places in Shakespeare.
43. *the knaves*] the great friends. Knave = young fellow, servant.
44. *ears*] ploughs: frequently used by Shakespeare and the Bible translators.
45. *in the crop*] bring in the crop. Rolfe quotes Bacon, *Henry VII.*, "All was inned at last into the King's barne." Holland's *Pliny*, "and when this is inned and laid up in the barne."
53. *Charbon . . . Poysam*] a reference to the lenten fare of puritan and papist. Malone is responsible for Poysam = Poisson. Benjamin Easy for Charbon = Chairbonne; he adds, "Shakespeare has clearly appropriated . . . the old French proverb '*Jeune chair et viel poisson.*' The full meaning intended to be conveyed is not that some, but that the best men, whatever their age or whatever may be their own or their wives' religion, all share the common fate." Malone understood "charbon" to be an allusion to the "firy zeal of the puritan."
55. *jowl*] knock. Cf. "How the knave jowls it to the ground." (*Hamlet,* v. i. 84). The word also occurs in North's "Plutarch" (*Theseus*), 2nd ed., 1595, p. 6.

Clo. A prophet I, madam; and I speak the truth the
next way: 60

> For I the ballad will repeat
> Which men full true shall find;
> Your marriage comes by destiny,
> Your cuckoo sings by kind.

Count. Get you gone, sir: I'll talk with you more 65
anon.
Stew. May it please you, madam, that he bid Helen
come to you: of her I am to speak.
Count. Sirrah, tell my gentlewoman I would speak
with her; Helen I mean. 70

Clo.   *Was this fair face the cause, quoth she,*
        Why the Grecians sacked Troy?
    Fond done, done fond,
        Was this King Priam's joy?

61-64.] Prose in the Ff; Rowe (ed. 2) first printed them as verse. 73, 74.] one line in Ff. After "fond done" Theobald (Warburton) inserts "for Paris he"; Capell conj. "but Paris he"; Collier, ed. 2 (MS.) "good sooth, it was"; Keightley "for only he"; Rann (Heath conj.) "For it undone, undone, quoth he." 74. joy?] ioy, F 1, 2; joy. (several modern editors).

59. *A prophet I*] Warburton comments as follows: "It is a supposition, which has run through all ages and people, that natural fools have something in them of divinity. On which account they were esteemed sacred; travellers tell us in what esteem the Turks now hold them; nor had they less honour (? irony) paid them heretofore in France, as appears from the old word *benet*, for a natural fool."

60. *next*] nearest. Cf. "'Tis the next way to turn tailor" (*1 Henry IV.* III. i. 264). The phrase is still used in Warwickshire, according to Henley.

61. ballad] Steevens points out that it is to be found in John Grange's *Garden* (1577).

64. by kind] in the nature of. Cf. "the worm will do his kind" (*Antony and Cleopatra*, v. ii. 264).

71-80.] stanza of an old ballad: a few words must have been lost. There seems to be no chance of correcting it, until the original is found. A ballad, ent. sta. reg. 1585, *The lamentation of Hecuba and the Ladyes of Troy* (Dr. Herford tells us), is lost. Warburton understood "ten" to refer to the ten sons of Priam.

> *With that she sighed as she stood,* 75
> *With that she sighed as she stood,*
> *And gave this sentence then;*
> *Among nine bad if one be good,*
> *Among nine bad if one be good,*
> *There's yet one good in ten.* 80

Count. What! one good in ten? you corrupt the song, sirrah.

Clo. One good woman in ten, madam; which is a purifying o' the song. Would God would serve the world so all the year! we'd find no fault with the 85 tithe-women if I were the parson. One in ten, quoth a'! An we might have a good woman born but or every blazing star, or at an earthquake, 'twould mend the lottery well: a man may draw his heart out ere a' pluck one. 90

Count. You'll be gone, sir knave, and do as I command you!

Clo. That man should be at woman's command, and yet no hurt done! Though honesty be no puritan, yet it will do no hurt; it will wear the 95

---

75. With ... stood] with ... stood, *bis* Ff. 76.] omitted in Ff and by Pope. 78–80.] Prose in Ff; verse by Rowe (ed. 2). 84. *o' the song*] Capell; *ath'* F 1, 2; *a' th* F 3, 4. 88. *or*] Capell; *ore* F 1, 2; *o're* F 3, 4; *o'er* Rowe; omitted Pope; *on* Rann; *ere* Collier (ed. 1); *one* Collier (ed. 2) MS.; *for* Harness; *'fore* Staunton. 90. *draw*] *pray* Rowe. 92. *you!*] *you?* Ff. 93. *woman's*] F 1; *a woman's* F 2, 3, 4. 93, 94. *and yet*] F 1, 2; *and get* F 3, 4. 94, 95. *no puritan*] *a puritan* Rann (Tyrwhitt conj.).

88. *or*] Capell's version. "For" is a likely alternative, but I see no reason for changing the original. Or=before.

89. *lottery well: a*] there may be a mistake in punctuation here. I prefer "lottery. Well, a ...".

90. *draw*] Rowe suggests "pray." I take "draw" in connection with lottery. A man may go on drawing and drawing till he dies, and not draw a good woman.

94, 95.] Dr. Herford writes: "Though honesty be no puritan, yet it will act as the puritans do; it will comply with the law outwardly in token of its humility, etc. The allusion

surplice of humility over the black gown of a big heart: I am going, forsooth: the business is for Helen to come hither. [*Exit.*

Count. Well, now.

Stew. I know, madam, you love your gentlewoman 100 entirely.

Count. Faith, I do: her father bequeathed her to me; and she herself, without other advantage, may lawfully make title to as much love as she finds: there is more owing her than is paid; and 105 more shall be paid her than she'll demand.

Stew. Madam, I was very late more near her than I think she wished me: alone she was, and did communicate to herself her own words to her own ears; she thought, I dare vow for her, they 110 touched not any stranger sense. Her matter was, she loved your son: Fortune, she said, was no goddess, that had put such difference betwixt their two estates; Love, no god, that would not extend his might, only where qualities were level; Dian, 115

115, 116. *level; Dian, no queen*] Globe ed. (Theobald's emendation); *levell, Queene* F 1, 2; *levell: Queen* F 3, 4; *level; . . . queen* Cambridge Edd. (thinking it probable that something more has been omitted, perhaps a whole line of the MS.).

is to the controversy touching such things as kneeling at the Communion, the ring in marriage, and especially the use of the surplice as an official vestment in the public services of the church. This controversy was running very high in the poet's time; all men were interested in it; so that the allusion would be generally understood. The puritans abominated the surplice as a rag of iniquity, and were great sticklers for the black gown, which was to them the symbol of Calvinism. Some of them, however, yielded so far as to wear the surplice over the gown, because their consciences would not suffer them to officiate without the latter, nor the law of the church without the former."

96. *big*] proud.

115. *qualities*] rank. "Gentlemen of blood and quality" (*Henry V.* IV. viii. 95).

115. *Dian . . .*] Theobald's well-known note runs as follows: "'Tis evident to every sensible reader that something must have slipt out here, by which the meaning of the context is rendered defective. The steward is speaking in the very words he overheard of the young lady; fortune was

no' queen of virgins, that would suffer her poor
knight surprised, without rescue in the first
assault or ransom afterward. This she delivered
in the most bitter touch of sorrow that e'er I
heard virgin exclaim in; which I held my duty 120
speedily to acquaint you withal, sithence in the
loss that may happen, it concerns you something
to know it.

Count. You have discharg'd this honestly; keep it to
yourself. Many likelihoods inform'd me of this 125
before, which hung so tottering in the balance,
that I could neither believe nor misdoubt. Pray
you, leave me: stall this in your bosom; and I
thank you for your honest care. I will speak
with you further anon. [*Exit Steward.* 130

Count. Even so it was with me when I was young:
 If ever we are nature's, these are ours; this thorn
 Doth to our rose of youth rightly belong;
 Our blood to us, this to our blood is born:

117. *knight surprised*] knight to be surprised Rowe.

no goddess, she said, for one reason; love, no god, for another;—what could she then more naturally subjoin, than as I have amended in the text: 'Diana, no queen . . .' For in poetical history, Diana was as well known to preside over chastity, as Cupid over love, or Fortune over the change or regulation of our circumstances." Boswell adds that "Diana's knight" is elsewhere used meaning "a virgin."

117. *surprised*] to be surprised. Dyce quotes Greene's *Penelope's Web* (1601), "suffering the princesse injury unrevenged." Dr. Herford quotes Drayton's *Harmonie of the Church* (1591), "suffer not their mouthes shut up, O Lord!"

119. *touch*] just above we have had "she thought (her words) touched not any stranger sense." Cf. also, "Did'st thou but know the inly touch of love" (*Two Gentlemen*, II. vii. 18). It is somewhat differently used in the expression, "One touch of nature makes the whole world kin," where the presence of the word nature makes it convey the sense of weakness.

121. *sithence*] sith, since.

128. *stall*] Shakespeare does not elsewhere use this word with a metaphorical sense.

133. *rose of youth*] "tell him he wears the rose Of youth upon him" (*Antony and Cleopatra*, III. xiii. 20).

134. *Our blood to us*] "This thorn is

It is the show and seal of nature's truth,   135
Where love's strong passion is impress'd in youth:
By our remembrances of days foregone,
Such were our faults; or then we thought them none.

Enter HELENA.

Her eye is sick on 't: I observe her now.
Hel. What is your pleasure, madam?   140
Count. You know, Helen, I am a mother to you.
Hel. Mine honourable mistress.
Count.   Nay, a mother:
Why not a mother? When I said "a mother,"
Methought you saw a serpent: what's in "mother"
That you start at it? I say, I am your mother;   145
And put you in the catalogue of those
That were enwombed mine: 'tis often seen
Adoption strives with nature, and choice breeds
A native slip to us from foreign seeds;
You ne'er oppress'd me with a mother's groan,   150
Yet I express to you a mother's care.
God's mercy, maiden! does it curd thy blood
To say I am thy mother? What's the matter,

---

139. Enter *Helena*] Singer. After line 130 in Ff.   141. *You . . . you*] Capell divides into two lines ending *Helen . . . to you.*   142, 143. *Nay, a mother . . . said "a mother,"*] in one line in Ff.

as natural a thing as blood." Blood = passion. "The brain may devise laws for the blood, but a hot temper leaps over a cold decree" (*Merchant of Venice*, I. ii. 19).
138. *faults; or*] Many editors have wanted to change this. It may stand; meaning "as far as we can remember those were our only faults—or, rather, we did not think them faults then."
139. *on 't*] of 't, as very often in Shakespeare.
149. *native slip*] choice breeds a slip (a grafting?) which becomes native to us, though sprung from foreign (stranger) seed.

3

That this distemper'd messenger of wet,
The many-colour'd Iris, round thine eye?   155
Why? that you are my daughter?
Hel.   That I am not.
Count. I say, I am your mother.
Hel.   Pardon, madam;
The Count Rousillon cannot be my brother:
I am from humble, he from honour'd name;
No note upon my parents, his all noble: 160
My master, my dear lord he is; and I
His servant live, and will his vassal die.
He must not be my brother.
Count.   Nor I your mother?
Hel. You are my mother, madam: would you were,—
So that my lord your son were not my brother,— 165
Indeed my mother! or were you both our mothers,
I care no more for than I do for heaven,
So I were not his sister. Can't no other,

163. *mother?*] Rowe (ed. 2), *mother.* Ff.   167. *I care ... heaven*] *I care no more for than you do, 'fore heaven* Becket conj.; *I'd care e'en more for't than I do for heaven* Keightley; *I care no more for than I do fear heaven* Gould conj.; Steevens adds [Aside] to the Ff reading.

154. *distemper'd*] contains an idea of "bad weather." Cf. *King John*, III. iv. 154, "No distempered day."
155. *Iris*] Cf. *As You Like It*, III. ii. 393, "a blue eye and sunken"—one of Rosalind's marks of a lover. Cf. also *Rape of Lucrece* (1586), "And round about her tear-distained eye, Blue circles stream'd, like rainbows in the sky." Rounds=surrounds. ". . . That rounds the mortal temples of a king" (Dyce). There is a reference to the shadow round eyes that are in love or sorrowful.
166. *both our*] of us both. A common construction in Shakespeare. *Cym-*

beline, v. v. 388, "your three motives" =the motives of you three. Marlowe writes, "I have sworn to frustrate both their hopes," and Sheridan, "Tell her 'tis all our ways."
167. *I care ... heaven*] Some sense can undoubtedly be cked out of this line: but I take it to be corrupt. The most likely emendation seems to be, "I'd care more for it than I do for heaven, So I were not his sister." Or perhaps it means, "*I fret* about that as little as I do about heaven." "Careful hours"=hours full of care.
168. *Can't no other*] can it not be otherwise.

But, I your daughter, he must be my brother?
Count. Yes, Helen, you might be my daughter-in-law. 170
God shield you mean it not! daughter and mother
So strive upon your pulse. What! pale again?
My fear hath catch'd your fondness: now I see
The mystery of your loneliness, and find
Your salt tears' head: now to all sense 'tis gross 175
You love my son: invention is asham'd,
Against the proclamation of thy passion,
To say thou dost not: therefore tell me true;
But tell me then, 'tis so; for, look, thy cheeks
Confess it, th' one to th' other; and thine eyes 180
See it so grossly shown in thy behaviours,
That in their kind they speak it: only sin
And hellish obstinacy tie thy tongue,
That truth should be suspected. Speak, is 't so?
If it be so, you have wound a goodly clew; 185
If it be not, forswear 't: howe'er, I charge thee,
As heaven shall work in me for thine avail,
To tell me truly.
Hel. Good madam, pardon me!
Count. Do you love my son?
Hel. Your pardon, noble mistress!

174. *loneliness*] Theobald, *loueliness* Ff.   175, 176. *gross You*] *grosse: You* Ff.   180. *th' one to th' other*] Knight; *'ton tooth to th'* F 1; *'ton to th'* F 2; *'tone to th'* F 3, 4.   186. *forswear't: howe'er*] *forsweare't how ere* F 1, 2.   187. *thine*] F 1; *mine* F 2, 3, 4.   188. *truly*] *true* Hanmer.

174. *loneliness*] The Ff read loueliness. The correction was made on Lord Ellesmere's copy of the Folio— an emendation which has been accepted by most editors.
175. *gross*] palpable. Falstaff's lies were "like their father, gross as a mountain, open, palpable" (*1 Henry IV.* II. iv. 250).
181. *grossly*] conspicuously.
185. *wound . . . clew*] Cf. *Proverbs of John Heywood* (1546, Sharman, p. 118), "In being your own foe you spin a fayre thread." (W. J. C.)

Count. Love you my son?
Hel. Do not you love him, madam? 190
Count. Go not about; my love hath in't a bond,
 Whereof the world takes note: come, come, disclose
 The state of your affection, for your passions
 Have to the full appeach'd.
Hel. Then, I confess,
 Here on my knee, before high heaven and you, 195
 That before you, and next unto high heaven,
 I love your son.
 My friends were poor, but honest; so's my love:
 Be not offended, for it hurts not him
 That he is lov'd of me: I follow him not 200
 By any token of presumptuous suit;
 Nor would I have him till I do deserve him;
 Yet never know how that desert should be.
 I know I love in vain, strive against hope;
 Yet in this captious and intenible sieve 205

196, 197.] As in Pope. Printed as one line in Ff. 205. *captious*] *cap'cious* Farmer (conj.), *copious* Jackson (conj.); *intenible*] intemible F 1.

194. *appeach'd*] informed against you. "I will appeach the villain" (*Richard II*, v. ii. 79). Also cf. *Speed Chronicle* (1611, p. 620a), "he was openly appeach'd for treason."
198. *friends*] relations.
205. *captious . . . sieve*] The full stop after "siue" in the Ff is clearly a misprint, and all seem agreed that "siue" means "sieve." What "captious and intenible" means is not so easy to decide. Dr. Herford explains it: "apt to receive but not to hold." Malone takes "captious" to mean "recipient"; and "intenible" = incapable of holding. Farmer and Schmidt connect "captious" with "capacious." Rolfe supports Malone's interpretation. Singer would have us take "captious" in the sense of the Latin *captiosus* (deceptive). The allusion, he says, may be to the story of the Danaïdes, which has been thus moralised: "These Virgins, who in the flower of their age pour water into pierced vessels which they can never fill, what is it but to be always bestowing our love on the ungrateful?". The quotation is admirable; but I cannot think "captious" = *captiosus*. Cotgrave gives *captieux* = captious, cavilling, too curious, *also* cautelous. This seems to support the meaning "ungrateful," but not the meaning "deceitful."

I still pour in the waters of my love,
And lack not to lose still. Thus, Indian-like,
Religious in mine error, I adore
The sun, that looks upon his worshipper,
But knows of him no more. My dearest madam, 210
Let not your hate encounter with my love
For loving where you do: but if yourself,
Whose aged honour cites a virtuous youth,
Did ever in so true a flame of liking
Wish chastely and love dearly, than your Dian 215
Was both herself and Love: O! then, give pity
To her, whose state is such, that cannot choose
But lend and give where she is sure to lose;
That seeks not to find that her search implies,
But riddle-like, lives sweetly where she dies. 220

Count. Had you not lately an intent, speak truly,
To go to Paris?

Hel. Madam, I had.

Count. Wherefore? tell true.

207. *lack*] *reck* Keightley conj.; *lose*] F 4; *loose* F 1, 2, 3; *love* Tyrwhitt conj.
214. *liking*] F 1; *living* F 2; *loving* F 3, 4.   223. *Madam*] omitted Hanmer;
224. *tell true*] omitted Steevens (conj.); S. Walker conjectures separate line.
Dyce gives that reading and places "tell true" in a line by itself.

207. *lose still*] probably "I lack not (do not cease) to lose still more 'waters of love' vainly poured out."

213. *aged honour cites*] Malone explains: "whose respectable conduct in age shows or proves that you were no less virtuous when young." Cf. "The morning rise doth cite each moving sense from idle rest" (*Pilgrim*, 195). "I need not cite him to it" (*Two Gentlemen*, II. iv. 85). "It cites us, brother, to the field" (*3 Henry VI.* II. i. 34). I prefer to understand "cite" to mean "urge on"—your aged honour urges on (is a good example to) a well-disposed young person.

220. *riddle-like*] secretly, like a riddle. The foregoing lines seem to have suggested the simile. Cf. "Though like the pestilence and old-fashioned love, riddlingly it catch men, and doth remove never, till it be starved" (Donne).

222.] If these short sentences are to be arranged in verse at all I think Walker and Dyce have the right version: "To go to Paris? *Hel.* Madam I had. *Count.* Wherefore? ‖ Tell true. ‖ *Hel.* I will," etc. But

Hel. I will tell truth;· by grace itself I' swear. 225
You know my father left me some prescriptions
Of rare and prov'd effects, such as his reading
And manifest experience had collected
For general sovereignty; and that he will'd me
In heedfull'st reservation to bestow them, 230
As notes, whose faculties inclusive were,
More than they were in note. Amongst the rest,
There is a remedy, approv'd, set down,
To cure the desperate languishings whereof
The king is render'd lost.

Count. This was your motive 235
For Paris, was it? Speak.

Hel. My lord your son made me to think of this;
Else Paris, and the medicine, and the king,
Had from the conversation of my thoughts
Haply been absent then.

Count. But think you, Helen, 240

225. *tell truth*] F 1; *tell true* F 2, 3, 4. 228. *manifest*] *manifold* Collier (ed. 2), Long MS. and Collier MS. and S. Walker (*Crit. Ex.* ii. 245). 231. *notes*] *cures* Gould conj. 235, 236.] Capell's arrangement. In one line in the folios. 236. *it? Speak*] Steevens; *it, speake?* Ff. 240. *Haply*] Pope, *Happily* Ff.

seeing that in this case we have an unfinished line it may be advisable to retain the Ff reading, though that broken line "Tell true" may imply the pause during which Helena hesitates and then suddenly replies, "I *will* tell truth . . ."

228. *manifest*] A doubtful reading. I like the emendation "manifold" (Coll. MS.). Manifest must mean, if anything, famous.

229. *general sovereignty*] universal remedy.

230. *bestow them*] lay up or stow. Cf. "And when he came to the Tower, he took them from their hand and bestowed them in the house" (2 Kings v. 24).

231. *notes*] "cures" is Gould's conjecture. Notes may be a misprint.

231. *inclusive*] including everything.

232. *in note*] written down. Perhaps "known."

233. *approv'd*] See note above, I. ii. 50.

235. *render'd*] represented. "I heard him speak of that same brother, and he did render him the most unnatural that liv'd 'mongst men" (*As You Like It*, IV. iii. 123).

If you should tender your supposed aid,
He would receive it? He and his physicians
Are of a mind; he, that they cannot help him,
They, that they cannot help. How shall they credit
A poor unlearned virgin, when the schools, 245
Embowell'd of their doctrine, have left off
The danger to itself?

Hel.   There's something in't,
More than my father's skill, which was the great'st
Of his profession. That his good receipt
Shall for my legacy be sanctified 250
By the luckiest stars in heaven: and, would your
    honour
But give me leave to try success, I'd venture
The well-lost life of mine on his grace's cure
By such a day and hour.

Count.   Dost thou believe't?
Hel. Ay, madam, knowingly. 255
Count. Why, Helen, thou shalt have my leave and love,
Means and attendants, and my loving greetings
To those of mine in court. I'll stay at home
And pray God's blessing into thy attempt.
Be gone to-morrow; and be sure of this, 260
What I can help thee to, thou shalt not miss.
           [*Exeunt.*

247. *itself*] Rowe, *itselfe.* Ff; *in't*] *hints* Hanmer (Warburton).   249. *profession. That*] *profession, that* Ff.   254. *day and hour*] *day, an houre* Ff.   257. *attendants*] *attendance* S. Walker conj.

243. *help*] cure. Cf. "It helps the head-ache, cough and tissick" (Beaumont and Fletcher, *Rollo*, II. ii. Song).

ACT II

SCENE I.—*Paris. The King's Palace.*

Flourish. Enter the KING, *with divers young Lords taking leave for the Florentine war;* BERTRAM, PAROLLES, *and Attendants.*

King. Farewell, young lord: these warlike principles
Do not throw from you: and you, my lord, farewell:
Share the advice betwixt you; if both gain all,
The gift doth stretch itself as 'tis receiv'd,
And is enough for both.

First Lord.   'Tis our hope, sir,   5
After well enter'd soldiers, to return
And find your grace in health.

King. No, no, it cannot be; and yet my heart

1, 2. *lord*] Hanmer, *lords* Ff.   3. *both gain all*] Johnson, *both gain, all* Ff.   5. First Lord] Rowe, Lord G. Ff.

young Lords] "Throughout this scene the two speakers whom Rowe and all subsequent editors have called 'First' and 'Second Lord' are called in the Ff 'Lord G.' and 'Lord E.' In all likelihood, as Capell has suggested, the parts were originally played by two actors whose names began respectively with G and E; and in fact, in the list of 'Principall Actors' prefixed to the first Folio we find the names of Gilburne, Goughe and Ecclestone. The same actors doubtless took the parts of the two gentlemen who bring the letter to Helena in the second Scene of Act III., and who in the stage-directions of the Folio are termed 'French G.' and 'French E.' The confusion of speakers in the dialogue at the close of III. vi. will be remedied if we suppose the Folio to have printed Cap. G. by mistake for Cap. E. in line 113 and Cap. E. for Cap. G. in lines 115, 121. 'Lord E.' appears again in IV. i, and 'Cap. G.' and 'Cap. E.' in IV. iii." (Camb. Edd. vol. iii. p. 260).

3. *if both gain all*] the reading of Ff "if both gain, all" is surely wrong. The king tells them to *share* the advice: but even if both parties take *all* the advice, it will stretch itself accordingly.

6. *well enter'd soldiers*] become out and out soldiers. "His pupil age man entered thus" (*Coriolanus*, II. ii. 103). *Eng. Dial. Dict.* gives "enter" as a hunting term, meaning to train or break in a hound, etc., to admit him into the regular pack.

Will not confess he owes the malady
That doth my life besiege. Farewell, young lords; 10
Whether I live or die, be you the sons
Of worthy Frenchmen: let higher Italy,
Those bated that inherit but the fall
Of the last monarchy, see that you come
Not to woo honour, but to wed it; when 15
The bravest questant shrinks, find what you seek,
That fame may cry you loud: I say, farewell.
Second Lord. Health, at your bidding, serve your majesty!
King. Those girls of Italy, take heed of them:
They say our French lack language to deny 20
If they demand: beware of being captives,
Before you serve.
Both.   Our hearts receive your warnings.
King. Farewell. [*To Bert.*] Come hither to me.
                                       [*Exit, in his chair.*

12. *higher*] *hired* Coleridge conj., *hirer* Bulloch conj.   13. *Those bated*] *Those bastards* Hanmer.   16. *questant*] F 1 ; *question* F 2, 3, 4 ; *quester* Collier MS.   23.] [to B.] Pope, [to attendants] Theobald, omitted Ff, [retires to a couch, attendants leading him] Capell, [Go backe] Collier MS.

9. *he*] stands for "it," referring to the heart.

9. *owes*] owns, as below, II. v. 81.

12, 13. *higher . . . inherit*] With regard to Hanmer's reading, it seems difficult to meet the objection that the king would hardly speak of these particular Italians as bastards, seeing that his knights were about to enlist in their ranks. More probably he means the nobility of Italy (not including those who won glory in the fall of the Roman Empire). This is the opinion of Delius. Cf. *Julius Cæsar*, II. i. 110, "the high (=perfect) east." Other editors have understood it to mean the further part of Italy where the Senoys and Florentines lived. See below, IV. iii. 43.

15, 16.] The reading given is Pope's.

The Ff have "to wed it, when the bravest questant shrinks": "questant" is a word not used again by Shakespeare: I know of no other instance of it. The later Ff give "question"—a possible but very unlikely reading, as the verb "to shrink" is not used by Shakespeare transitively with the meaning "to shirk." If "question" is right, it means "duel," as in *Othello*, I. iii. 23. In *King Lear*, III. vii. 17, we find "knights . . . Hot questrists after him."

17. *cry you loud*] Cf. Beaumont and Fletcher, *The Hun. Lieut.*, II. i. 1, "when all men cry him" (*New Eng. Dict.*).

23. *Come hither to me*] There are no stage instructions in the Ff: to supply

First Lord. O my sweet lord, that you will stay behind us!
Par. 'Tis not his fault, the spark.
Second Lord. O! 'tis brave wars. 25
Par. Most admirable: I have seen those wars.
Ber. I am commanded here, and kept a coil with
"Too young," and "the next year," and "'tis too early."
Par. An thy mind stand to 't, boy, steal away bravely.
Ber. I shall stay here the forehorse to a smock, 30
Creaking my shoes on the plain masonry,
Till honour be bought up, and no sword worn
But one to dance with. By heaven! I'll steal away.

29. *An . . . bravely*] Theobald; *And . . . too 't boy, steale away bravely* F 1, 2, 3; *And thy mind—Stand to it, boy; steal away bravely.* Pope.

them is by no means easy. Pope makes the king leave the stage; Capell supposes that he retires to a couch. Mr. P. A. Daniel supposes that the king is conveyed to a couch at the back of the stage and that a traverse is drawn before him; this is perhaps the only satisfactory view. Theobald would make the king tell *the attendants* to come to him: surely it is Bertram whom he summons; B. moves to obey when the First Lord exclaims "That you will stay behind!" The crux is Bertram's "Stay the king" (line 49). These words probably mean that he is going to stay with or support the king. I cannot think that they can have any reference to the reappearance of the King. Mr. P. A. Daniel would adopt Pope's emendation "Stay; the king—" meaning "I am going to stay. The king —(with a shrug) will have it so." The Cambridge Editors give the reading of the later Ff, "Stay: the king." Explaining: "The king we may suppose is carried out on a couch. When Bertram says 'Stay: the king,' the ushers in attendance throw open the folding doors at the back of the stage, Bertram and Parolles retire close to one of the side doors, and while they are speaking together the king is borne in upon his couch to the front of the stage. . . . We must . . . suppose that he is reclining on a couch throughout the whole scene. Thus at his first appearance, his illness would be made evident to the spectators. After they have set the couch down, the attendants retire to the back of the stage so as to be out of earshot."

30. *forehorse . . .*] the horse in a team which goes foremost. "I'll learn you the names of all our team and acquaint you with Jock the forehorse and Fibb the fill-horse" (T. Heywood's *Fortune by Land and Sea*). Bertram refers to ushering in squiring ladies (Schmidt). Delius takes it to mean a linen-horse.

32. *Till . . . bought up*] till there is no honour left to be gained (Schmidt).

32, 33. *sword . . . to dance with*] Men used to wear short swords for dancing, a custom frequently referred to in literature. It is called a "dancing-rapier." in *Titus Andronicus*, II. i. 39. Cf. also *Antony and Cleopatra*, III. xi. 36.

First Lord. There's honour in the theft.
Par. Commit it, count.
Second Lord. I am your accessary; and so farewell. 35
Ber. I grow to you, and our parting is a tortured body.
First Lord. Farewell, captain.
Second Lord. Sweet Monsieur Parolles!
Par. Noble heroes, my sword and yours are kin.
Good sparks and lustrous, a word, good metals: 40
you shall find in the regiment of the Spinii one
Captain Spurio, with his cicatrice, an emblem of
war, here on his sinister cheek: it was this very
sword entrenched it: say to him, I live, and
observe his reports for me. 45
Second Lord. We shall, noble captain. [*Exeunt Lords.*
Par. Mars dote on you for his novices! [*To Bert.*]
What will you do?
Ber. Stay the king.
Par. Use a more spacious ceremony to the noble 50

42. *with . . . emblem*] Theobald, *his cicatrice* (sicatrice F 1), *with an emblem* Ff.   47. [To Bert.] Capell, omitted Ff.   48. *you*] Capell, *ye* Ff.   49. *Stay the king*] F 1; *Stay: the king* F 2, 3, 4; *Stay; the king*— Pope.

36. *tortured body*] Cf. the use of the word body in "the body of your discourse is sometime guarded with fragments" (*Much Ado*, I. i. 287). It is here used meaning nothing more than "thing." This strange (and somewhat foolish) manner of farewell has been thought corrupt: but I think the reading of the Ff may stand.

48. *What will you do?*] Capell's reading. Ff have "ye." To whom is this addressed? Capell thinks to Bertram. If so, does Bertram answer, "I will stay the king," or does he interrupt (as most editors take it) by calling attention to the entrance of the king? I think the former. Mr. Daniel writes: "The scene ends line 61 with the departure of Bertram and Parolles. Perhaps we ought now to mark a new scene; but it would necessitate renumbering the lines and cause confusion. The traverse is now withdrawn, discovering Lafeu kneeling before him. On the old stage the king would probably be brought forward in his chair, just as he was conveyed out at line 23." The Cambridge Editors, on the other hand, say: "as printed in the Ff the words 'what will ye do?' seem to be a taunt addressed, after the speaker's manner, to the young lords when their backs were turned."

49. *Stay the king*] be in attendance on him. See Cotgrave, "*Supporter=* to support, sustain, stay or beare up."

lords; you have restrained yourself within the
list of too cold an adieu: be more expressive to
them; for they wear themselves in the cap of the
time, there do muster true gait, eat, speak, and
move under the influence of the most received 55
star; and though the devil lead the measure,
such are to be followed. After them, and take a
more dilated farewell.

Ber. And I will do so.

Par. Worthy fellows; and like to prove most sinewy 60
sword-men.   [*Exeunt Bertram and Parolles.*

Re-enter KING *in his chair and* LAFEU.

Laf. Pardon, my lord, for me and for my tidings.

King. I'll fee thee to stand up.

Laf. Then here's a man stands that has brought his
pardon.

I would you had kneel'd, my lord, to ask me mercy, 65
And that at my bidding you could so stand up.

King. I would I had; so I had broke thy pate,

---

54. *gait*] Johnson, *gate* Ff.   55. *move*] F 1; *more* F 2, 3, 4.   63. *fee*] Theobald, *see* Ff.   64. *brought*] *bought* Theobald.   67. and fol. arranged as in Capell.

54. *there . . . gait*] there (in the cap of time) true gait (those who are fashionable) do muster or come together.
56. *measure*] dance.
61.] Pope makes this the beginning of Scene ii. And he is probably right. But it is difficult to change what has practically become an accepted division of this Act (into five Scenes).
63. *fee thee to stand up*] This seems to be an unusual way of saying, "I'll fee thee if thou can'st make me stand up." I know of no instance of the verb "fee" used with "to," but in Fielding's *The Mock Doctor*, II. iii., there occurs, "I'll fee you, you villain —cure me!" where it evidently means "I'll give you your fee—but cure me." In the present instance the king must have meant, "I'll fee thee if I stand up," to which Lafeu immediately replies, "Then here's a man has brought his pardon." Some editors give "bought." But the pardon is clearly defined by what follows—"'tis thus."

<blockquote>

And ask'd thee mercy for 't.
Laf.   Good faith, across.
But, my good lord, 'tis thus; will you be cur'd
Of your infirmity?
King.   No.
Laf.   O! will you eat   70
No grapes, my royal fox? Yes, but you will
My noble grapes an if my royal fox
Could reach them. I have seen a medicine
That's able to breathe life into a stone,
Quicken a rock, and make you dance canary   75
With spritely fire and motion; whose simple touch
Is powerful to araise King Pepin, nay,
To give great Charlemain a pen in 's hand
And write to her a love-line.
King.   What "her" is this?
Laf. Why, Doctor She.   My lord, there's one arriv'd,   80
If you will see her: now, by my faith and honour,
If seriously I may convey my thoughts
In this my light deliverance, I have spoke

</blockquote>

68. *Good faith, across*] not a brilliant retort. The metaphor is taken from the tournaments; it was considered shameful to break a lance "across" your opponent "like a noble goose" (*As You Like It*, III. iv. 47).

72. *My noble grapes*] Rolfe points out that the "my" is emphatic. There is perhaps a reference to Æsop's Fable.

73. *medicine*] physician. Cotgrave uses the word in the same way. See also *Winter's Tale*, IV. iv. 597; *Macbeth*, V. ii. 27.

75. *dance canary*] to dance a lively jig. The origin of the word "canary" seems obscure, but it may have something to do with the wine.

77. *araise*] an old form which occurs in *Morte d'Arthur*, and frequently elsewhere (see *New Eng. Dict.*).

77. *King Pepin*] a name chosen because he had been dead some time: in *Love's Labour's Lost*, IV. i., we hear of "one that was a man when King Pepin was a little boy."

79.] It has been pointed out that this sentence is not grammatically correct; but it is, logically, and I cannot think that a whole line can have been lost. Shakespeare was fond of these elliptical constructions. Capell would read "and give . . . hand To write." It will be remembered that Charlemagne could not write.

83. *light deliverance*] jesting manner of speaking (W. J. C.).

With one, that in her sex, her years, profession,
Wisdom and constancy, hath amaz'd me more   85
Than I dare blame my weakness.   Will you see her,
For that is her demand, and know her business?
That done, laugh well at me.

King.   Now, good Lafeu,
Bring in the admiration, that we with thee
May spend our wonder too, or take off thine   90
By wond'ring how thou took'st it.

Laf.   Nay, I'll fit you,
And not be all day neither.   [*Exit.*

King. Thus he his special nothing ever prologues.

Re-enter LAFEU, *with* HELENA.

Laf. Nay, come your ways.
King.   This haste hath wings indeed.
Laf. Nay, come your ways.   95
   This is his majesty, say your mind to him:
   A traitor you do look like; but such traitors
   His majesty seldom fears: I am Cressid's uncle,
   That dare leave two together.   Fare you well.
                                                [*Exit.*
King. Now, fair one, does your business follow us?   100
Hel. Ay, my good lord.   Gerard de Narbon was

---

86. *blame*] *blaze* Theobald conj., *task* Keightley conj.   100. *follow*] *fellow* Anon. conj.   101. and fol. arranged as in Hanmer.

84. *profession*] what she professed to be or to be able to do; "her demand and her business" (line 87).   Cf. "It is the privilege of mine honours, my oath and my profession" (*King Lear*, v. iii. 130).

86. *blame my weakness*] more than I dare confess.
89. *admiration*] a wonder.
91. *I'll fit you*] satisfy you.
100. *follow us?*] Cf. "the liberty that follows our places" (*Henry V.* v. ii. 297).

My father; in what he did profess, well found.
King. I knew him.
Hel. The rather will I spare my praises towards him;
Knowing him is enough. On's bed of death   105
Many receipts he gave me; chiefly one,
Which, as the dearest issue of his practice,
And of his old experience the only darling,
He bade me store up as a triple eye,
Safer than mine own two, more dear. I have
so;   110
And, hearing your high majesty is touch'd
With that malignant cause wherein the honour
Of my dear father's gift stands chief in power,
I come to tender it and my appliance,
With all bound humbleness.
King.   We thank you, maiden; 115
But may not be so credulous of cure,
When our most learned doctors leave us, and
The congregated college have concluded
That labouring art can never ransom nature
From her inaidable state; I say we must not   120
So stain our judgment, or corrupt our hope,
To prostitute our past-cure malady
To empirics, or to dissever so

106. *chiefly*] *namely* F 3, 4.   110. *two, more dear.*] stops substantially as in Steevens; *two: more deare* Ff.   120. *inaidable*] Capell; *inaydible* F 1, 2; *unaydible* F 3, 4; *state*] Dyce (ed. 2) (S. Walker conj.), *estate* Ff.

102. *well found*] Steevens explains "of known, acknowledged excellence." Delius understands it to mean "learned."
109. *triple*] used more than once by Shakespeare to mean "third." Cf. *Antony and Cleopatra*, I. i. 12.

112. *cause*] "disease, sickness. 1509, Hawes, *Past. Pleas.* xviii., xvii., 'I your cause can nothing remedy.' 1578, Lyte, *Dodoeus*, III. xxvi.353, 'Hellebor may not be ministred except in desperate causes.' Cf. *Coriolanus*, III. i. 235" (*New Eng. Dict.*).

                Our great self and our credit, to esteem
                A senseless help, when help past sense we deem. 125
Hel. My duty then shall pay me for my pains:
                I will no more enforce mine office on you;
                Humbly entreating from your royal thoughts
                A modest one, to bear me back again.
King. I cannot give thee less, to be call'd grateful. 130
                Thou thought'st to help me; and such thanks I give
                As one near death to those that wish him live;
                But what at full I know, thou know'st no part,
                I knowing all my peril, thou no art.
Hel. What I can do can do no hurt to try, 135
                Since you set up your rest 'gainst remedy.
                He that of greatest works is finisher,
                Oft does them by the weakest minister:
                So holy writ in babes hath judgment shown,
                When judges have been babes; great floods have flown 140
                From simple sources; and great seas have dried
                When miracles have by the great'st been denied.

125. *help*] cure, as often in Shakespeare. See below, II. iii. 16. Also *Two Gentlemen*, "help him of his blindness" (in *Who is Sylvia?*).

136. *set up your rest*] Professor Dowden says it is "a metaphor from primero (a game at cards); the *stake* was a smaller sum, the *rest* a larger sum, which, if a player were confident (or desperate) might all be *set* or *set up*, that is, wagered." In the game of primero played in dialogue (in the Dialogues (p. 26) appended to Minsheu's *Spanish Dict.*) "two shillings form the stake, eight shillings the rest. . . ." Cotgrave has under *Renvier*: "*Il y renvioit de sa reste*, He set his whole rest, he adventured all his estate upon it." Hence to set up one's rest came to mean to be determined, resolved. For many examples, see Nares' *Glossary*. See also *Romeo and Juliet*, IV. v. 6 (and others).

140. *judges have been babes*] Holt White supposes that Shakespeare referred to the story of Susanna and Daniel. On the other hand, Malone thinks the passage refers to Christ's well-known words.

142. *by the great'st*] "by" is here used as in the phrase "he did his duty by his children."

Oft expectation fails, and most oft there
Where most it promises; and oft it hits
Where hope is coldest and despair most fits. 145
King. I must not hear thee: fare thee well, kind maid.
Thy pains, not us'd, must by thyself be paid:
Proffers not took reap thanks for their reward.
Hel. Inspired merit so by breath is barr'd.
It is not so with him that all things knows, 150
As 'tis with us that square our guess by shows;
But most it is presumption in us when
The help of heaven we count the act of men,
Dear sir, to my endeavours give consent;
Of heaven, not me, make an experiment. 155
I am not an impostor that proclaim
Myself against the level of mine aim;
But know I think, and think I know most sure,
My art is not past power nor you past cure.
King. Art thou so confident? Within what space 160
Hop'st thou my cure?
Hel. The great'st grace lending grace,

143.] Johnson believes that a line has dropt out here, because there is nothing to rhyme with "there." 145. *fits*] Collier (Theobald conj.), *shifts* Ff. 156. *impostor*] F 3, 4; *impostrue* F 1, 2; *imposture* Capell. 161. *The great'st . . . grace*] Capell, *The greatest grace lending grace* Ff, *The greatest lending grace* Rowe.

145. *fits*] The Ff read "shifts." On the margin of the copy in Lord Ellesmere's possession, the correction "fits" has been made. Theobald suggested the same emendation.

149. *by breath is barr'd*] bar = to prevent or keep out. "Merriment which bars a thousand harms" (*Taming of the Shrew*, Induction, ii. 138). "Breath" = (probably) language, word, —as in *Measure for Measure*, v. 122, "permit A blasting and a scandalous breath to fall on him."

151. *square our guess by shows*] Cf. "thou art said to have a stubborn soul, that apprehends no further than this world, and squarest thy life according" (*Measure for Measure*, v. 487).

156, 157. *proclaim . . . mine aim*] To proclaim one thing against another is to say that it is better or superior to it. Helen says, "Myself (my power) which I proclaim is not inferior to (or unable to attain) the high level of my aim."

161. *The . . . grace*] The Ff read "the greatest grace lending grace."

50 ALL'S WELL [ACT II.

 Ere twice the horses of the sun shall bring
 Their fiery torcher his diurnal ring,
 Ere twice in murk and occidental damp
 Moist Hesperus hath quench'd her sleepy lamp 165
 Or four-and-twenty times the pilot's glass
 Hath told the thievish minutes how they pass,
 What is infirm from your sound parts shall fly,
 Health shall live free, and sickness freely die.
King. Upon thy certainty and confidence 170
 What dar'st thou venture?
Hel. Tax of impudence,
 A strumpet's boldness, a divulged shame,
 Traduc'd by odious ballads: my maid's name
 Sear'd otherwise; ne worse of worst, extended

173. *maid's name*] S. Walker conj., *maiden's name* Ff. 174. *ne worse of worst*] Ff, *nay, worse, if worse, extended* Anon. conj., *on worst of racks extended* Anon. conj. The later Ff have "no" instead of "ne."

Most editors give "great'st." But the line "Hopest thou my cure? The great'st grace lending grace" is impossible: it is difficult to believe Shakespeare wrote it. Mr. Craig writes and says, "Suppose that Shakespeare wrote first, 'The great God lending grace,' and that, on account of the Act against profanity on the stage, the players were induced to alter this and instead of 'God' put 'grace.' Then finding that 'the great Grace' did not sound well they may have decided to read 'the great'st grace lending grace.'" Delius quotes *Macbeth*, v. vii., "by the grace of Grace."

164. *in murk*] this word may here be either a noun or an adjective: it matters little which of the two.

165. *her*] most editors correct this to "his." But the "mistake" was possibly in the original MS., and it is as well to leave it.

166. *pilot's glass*] technically half an hour. Not so used by Shakespeare. (See *Shakespeare and Sea-Glasses*, by Dr. Brinsley Nicholson, *New Sh. Soc. Tr.*, March 12, 1880.)

171. *Tax*] accusation.

174. *ne*] and not. By "ne worse of worst" Helena probably means that nothing could be worse than "my name sear'd otherwise." *extended* = seized by a course of law. Johnson (*Dict.*) quotes Hudibras: "The law that settles all you do, And marries where you did but woo; An(d) if it judge upon your side, Will soon extend her for your bride; And put her person, goods or lands, Or which you like best, int' your hands." Cf. also *As You Like It*, III. i. 17, "Let my officers make an extent upon his house and land, And turn him going." Also, *Antony and Cleopatra*, I. ii. 105, "Labienus hath extended Asia."—The Cambridge Editors cite more than twenty various readings of this phrase.

  With vilest torture let my life be ended.   175
King. Methinks in thee some blessed spirit doth speak
  His powerful sound within an organ weak;
  And what impossibility would slay
  In common sense, sense saves another way.
  Thy life is dear; for all that life can rate   180
  Worth name of life in thee hath estimate;
  Youth, beauty, wisdom, courage, . . . all
  That happiness and prime can happy call:
  Thou this to hazard needs must intimate
  Skill infinite or monstrous desperate.   185
  Sweet practiser, thy physic I will try,
  That ministers thine own death if I die.
Hel. If I break time, or flinch in property
  Of what I spoke, unpitied let me die,
  And well deserv'd. Not helping, death's my fee; 190
  But, if I help, what do you promise me?
King. Make thy demand.

---

 175. *vilest*] *vildest* F 1, 2.   182. *courage . . . all*] *courage, all* Ff. Two syllables seem to have been left out here, perhaps "health and." Theobald supplies "virtue," Collier "honour."   183. *happiness and*] *happiness in* Rann (Mason conj.).

 177. *powerful sound*] direct object of "speak."
 178, 179. *what . . . another way*] There's sense in what you say, but it is not *common* sense.
 181. *in thee hath estimate*] Hath great value in a young life like yours.
 183. *happiness and prime*] Why change to "happiness in prime" as Rann and Mason conjecture? Because "in the prime" is the trite phrase? This use of the word "prime" is as beautiful as the one in which Shakespeare says, "love is crowned with the prime in spring time."

 185. *monstrous desperate*] a strange construction. Desperate seems to agree with "a disposition" understood. The meaning is quite clear.
 188, 189. *property Of what*] "in property of" does not seem to have been a usual construction at any time. Shakespeare speaks of "property of blood," meaning probably "right." Milton uses the word "proper" meaning "original" in the phrase "our proper motion." Perhaps the sentence here means, "If I flinch in the exact fulfilment of the conditions, I have accepted. . . ."

Hel. But will you make it even?

King. Ay, by my sceptre, and my hopes of heaven.

Hel. Then shalt thou give me with thy kingly hand
What husband in thy power I will command: 195
Exempted be from me the arrogance
To choose from forth the royal blood of France,
My low and humble name to propagate
With any branch or image of thy state;
But such a one, thy vassal, whom I know 200
Is free for me to ask, thee to bestow.

King. Here is my hand; the premises observ'd,
Thy will by my performance shall be serv'd:
So make the choice of thy own time, for I,
Thy resolv'd patient, on thee still rely. 205
More should I question thee, and more I must,
Though more to know could not be more to trust,
From whence thou cam'st, how tended on; but rest
Unquestion'd welcome and undoubted blest.
Give me some help here, ho! If thou proceed 210
As high as word, my deed shall match thy deed.

[*Flourish. Exeunt.*

193. *heaven*] Theobald (Thirlby conj.), *help(e)* Ff. 199. *image*] *impage* (Warburton).

193. *hopes of heaven*] Ff have "helpe" instead of "heaven." As Boswell points out, the only reason for changing what is perfect sense is the break in the rhyme; the reason is sufficiently conclusive here.

199. *image of thy state*] Warburton's emendation "impage" is beautiful:

but he gives no instance of the use of this word: it seems rare. Henley says that "*branch* refers to the collateral descendants of the royal blood, and *image* to the direct and immediate line."

201. *bestow*] See note on II. iii. 55, below.

SCENE II.—*Rousillon. A Room in the Countess's Palace.*

Enter COUNTESS *and Clown.*

Count. Come on, sir; I shall now put you to the height of your breeding.

Clo. I will show myself highly fed and lowly taught. I know my business is but to the court.

Count. To the court! why, what place make you 5 special, when you put off that with such contempt? "But to the court!"

Clo. Truly, madam, if God have lent a man any manners, he may easily put it off at court: he that cannot make a leg, put off's cap, kiss his 10 hand, and say nothing, has neither leg, hands, lip, nor cap; and indeed such a fellow, to say precisely, were not for the court. But for me, I have an answer will serve all men.

Count. Marry, that's a bountiful answer that fits all 15 questions.

Clo. It is like a barber's chair that fits all buttocks; the pin-buttock, the quatch-buttock, the brawn buttock, or any buttock.

6, 7. *contempt? . . . court!*] Pope, *contempt, . . . court?* Ff.   13. *court, But*] Rowe, *court, but* Ff.

10, 11. *cannot . . . say nothing*] cannot say anything.
10. *make a leg*] a common phrase; cf. Ben Jonson's *Cynthia's Revels*, "Hath travelled to make legs and seen the cringe Of several courts" (W. J. C.).
17. *like a barber's chair*] proverbial (see Ray's Proverbs. Burton's *Anatomy of Melancholy*, ed. 1632, p. 666).

Steevens quotes from *More Fooles Yet* by R. S.—1610, 4to: "Moreover sattin sutes he doth compare Unto the service of a barber's chayre; As fit for every Jacke and journeyman As for a knight or worthy gentleman."
18. *quatch*] fat and squat (probably). I know of no other instance of this word.

Count. Will your answer serve fit to all questions? 20
Clo. As fit as ten groats is for the hand of an attorney, as your French crown for your taffeta punk, as Tib's rush for Tom's forefinger, as a pancake for Shrove-Tuesday, a morris for Mayday, as the nail to his hole, the cuckold to his 25 horn, as a scolding quean to a wrangling knave, as the nun's lip to the friar's mouth; nay, as the pudding to his skin.
Count. Have you, I say, an answer of such fitness for all questions? 30
Clo. From below your duke to beneath your constable, it will fit any question.
Count. It must be an answer of most monstrous size that must fit all demands.
Clo. But a trifle neither, in good faith, if the learned 35 should speak truth of it. Here it is, and all that belongs to 't: ask me if I am a courtier; it shall do you no harm to learn.
Count. To be young again, if we could. I will be

20. *serve fit to*] suit, fit. Cf. "How fit his garments serve me!" (*Cymbeline*, IV. i. 2).

21. *ten groats*] a piece of money worth 3s. 4d.—the attorney's fee.

22. *French crown*] there is probably a reference to "Morbus Gallicus"—the joke was a favourite one (see *Midsummer Night's Dream*, I. ii. 99).

22, 23. *taffeta punk*] strumpet dressed in taffeta. French crown= her price. There is an old proverb, "All that the Clarke toyles for his Punke devours."

23. *Tib's . . . forefinger*] Sir J. Hawkins says that "Tom is the man and Tib the woman; therefore, more properly, we might read—Tom's rush for Tib's finger." But it is of small importance. "Rush" is probably a reference to the old custom (or abuse) of putting a rush ring on the finger of a woman about to marry *de facto* but not *de jure*. (See Brand's *Popular Antiquities*, Bohn's ed. 2, 107.)

24. *morris*] "a mayday frolic, with dancing and a hobby-horse performance: originally called morisco, and said to be derived from the Moors through Spain, where it is still popular under the name of *fandango*" (Dr. Herford). Cf. the game of Nine men's morris (*Midsummer Night's Dream*, II. i. 98).

39. *young again, if we could*] "The

a fool in question, hoping to be the wiser by 40
your answer. I pray you, sir, are you a courtier?
Clo. O Lord, sir! there's a simple putting off.
More, more, a hundred of them.
Count. Sir, I am a poor friend of yours, that loves you.
Clo. O Lord, sir! Thick, thick, spare not me. 45
Count. I think, sir, you can eat none of this homely
meat.
Clo. O Lord, sir! Nay, put me to't, I warrant you.
Count. You were lately whipped, sir, as I think.
Clo. O Lord, sir! Spare not me. 50
Count. Do you cry, "O Lord, sir!" at your whipping,
and "spare not me"? Indeed your "O Lord,
sir!" is very sequent to your whipping: you
would answer very well to a whipping, if you
were but bound to't. 55
Clo. I ne'er had worse luck in my life in my "O
Lord, sir!" I see things may serve long, but
not serve ever.
Count. I play the noble housewife with the time,
To entertain 't so merrily with a fool. 60
Clo. O Lord, sir! why, there 't serves well again.
Count. An end, sir: to your business. Give Helen this,

41. *I pray*] F 3; *La. I pray* . . . F 1, 2; *Lady. I pray* . . . F 4. 59, 60.] Prose in Ff; verse by Knight. 60. *entertain't*] Cambridge Edd. (S. Walker conj.), *entertain it* Ff. 62. *An end, sir: to*] Rowe (ed. 2); *And end sir to* F 1, 2; *And end; sir to* F 3, 4.

lady censures her own levity in trifling with her jester, as a ridiculous attempt to return back to youth" (Johnson). "To be" is dependent on the clown's "to learn" (Cowden Clarke).
42. *O Lord, sir*] Warburton calls this "that foolish expletive of speech then in vogue at court." It was ridiculed by other writers.
45. *thick*] quick. Cf. *Cymbeline*, III. ii. 58, "Say and speak thick." *Troilus and Cressida*, III. ii. 38, "my heart beats thicker than a feverish pulse."

And urge her to a present answer back:
Commend me to my kinsmen and my son.
This is not much. 65
Clo. Not much commendation to them.
Count. Not much employment for you: you under-
stand me?
Clo. Most fruitfully: I am there before my legs.
Count. Haste you again. [*Exeunt severally.* 70

SCENE III.—*Paris. A Room in the King's Palace.*

Enter BERTRAM, LAFEU, *and* PAROLLES.

Laf. They say miracles are past; and we have our
philosophical persons, to make modern and
familiar, things supernatural and causeless.
Hence is it that we make trifles of terrors, ensconcing ourselves into seeming knowledge, when we 5
should submit ourselves to an unknown fear.
Par. Why, 'tis the rarest argument of wonder that
hath shot out in our latter times.

---

66. *them*] *them?* Theobald conj.   68. *me?*] Capell, *me.* Ff.

66. *Not . . . them*] may be a question as Theobald conjectured. But it is just as well as it is.

Scene III.

2, 3. *modern and familiar*] See Act v. iii. 216, below, "with her modern grace." Also *As You Like It*, II. vii. 156, "Full of wise saws and modern instances." "Modern" occurs frequently (ten times) in Shakespeare, and in this case means "common, everyday."

3. *causeless*] "having no antecedent cause, fortuitous (*New Eng. Dict.*).

4, 5. *ensconcing ourselves into*] an instance of the use of a verb of rest with into. Literally "retire into a sconce or fortification." It is thus used by Rowley in *A Match at Midnight*, "Look an he hath not esconced himself" (Dods. Old Plays, Hazl. vol. xiii. p. 47). W. J. C. Cf. *Sonnets*, xlix., "Against that time do I insconce me here Within the knowledge of mine own desert."

6. *an unknown fear*] one of Shakespeare's beautiful metonymies.

7. *argument*] subject. Cf. "The argument of your praise" (*King Lear*, I. i. 218); see also *Much Ado*, II. iii. 11, and below, III. v. 60.

Ber. And so 'tis.
Laf. To be relinquished of the artists,— 10
Par. So I say, both of Galen and Paracelsus.
Laf. Of all the learned and authentic fellows,—
Par. Right; so I say.
Laf. That gave him out incurable,—
Par. Why, there 'tis; so say I too. 15
Laf. Not to be help'd,—
Par. Right; as 'twere a man assured of a—
Laf. Uncertain life, and sure death.
Par. Just; you say well: so would I have said.
Laf. I may truly say it is a novelty to the world. 20
Par. It is, indeed: if you will have it in showing, you shall read it in — what do you call there?
Laf. A showing of a heavenly effect in an earthly actor 25
Par. That's it; I would have said the very same.

11.] The Cambridge Editors suggest giving the words "*both* ... *Paracelsus*" to Lafeu and adding another "Par. *So I say.*" This reading has been adopted in the Globe and Oxford editions. 21. *It is, indeed: if*] *it is indeede if* Ff. 22. *in—what*] Capell, *in what* Ff. 23. *there?*] Capell, *there.* Ff. 26. *That's it; I ... said the*] *That's it, I ... said, the* F 1, 2, 3; *That's it, I ... said; the* Capell.

10. *artists*] used only a few times by Shakespeare and always in the sense of "scholars." The universities still use the word "arts" in the same way.

11. *Galen and Paracelsus*] Galen, A.D. 130-200 (?) Paracelsus, 1493-1541 —two names usually linked together and familiar to all, as representing medicine generally.

12. *authentic*] original; perhaps duly qualified, licensed. Cf. 1540, Act 32 Henry VIII., xxv., "With the approbacions and testimonies of fowre sundrie notaries authentique thereunto subscribed." 1610, BenJonson, *Alch.* II. iii., "Why, h' is the most authentique dealer in these commodities" (*New Eng. Dict.*). The author of *Was Shakespeare a Lawyer?* sees here a reference to the recognised members of the College of Physicians which first received a charter from Edward VI. (?)

16. *help'd*] cured, as above, II. i. 125.

21. *in showing*] on paper.

24, 25. *A showing ... actor*] Warburton says that this must be the title of some pamphlet here ridiculed.

Laf. Why, your dolphin is not lustier: 'fore me, I speak in respect—
Par. Nay, 'tis strange, 'tis very strange, that is the brief and the tedious of it; and he's of a most facinerious spirit that will not acknowledge it to be the— 30
Laf. Very hand of heaven—
Par. Ay, so I say.
Laf. In a most weak— 35
Par. And debile minister, great power, great transcendence: which should, indeed, give us a further use to be made than alone the recovery of the king, as to be—
Laf. Generally thankful. 40
Par. I would have said it: you say well. Here comes the king.

Enter KING, HELENA, *and Attendants.*

Laf. Lustig, as the Dutchman says: I'll like a maid the better, whilst I have a tooth in my head. Why, he's able to lead her a carranto. 45

35-40.] There are various readings. The passage may be corrupt. 43. *Lustig*] *Lustique* F 1, 2.

27. *dolphin*] "a plain fish." Cf. *Antony and Cleopatra*, v. ii. 88, "His delights Were dolphin like." In Holland's *Pliny* (a book Shakespeare read) the dolphin is described as being "the swiftest of all other living creatures, and not of sea-fish only . . . quicker than the flying fowl . . . disporteth himself and fetcheth a thousand friskes and gamboles" (W. J. C.).

31. *facinerious*] Parolles' mistake for "facinorous," a word meaning wicked.

43. *Lustig*] A Dutch word used by English writers of that time. Steevens gives two instances from works dated 1618 and 1634 (respectively), namely, "can walk a mile or two as lustique as a boor."—"what! all lustick, all frolicksome!"

45. *carranto*] a coranto = lively dance. See *Twelfth Night*, I. iii. 137, and *Henry V.* III. v. 33. Johnson calls it "cor'ant, a lofty sprightly dance, from French *courant*" (it used to be spelled "couranto").

Par. Mor du vinager! Is not this Helen?
Laf. 'Fore God, I think so.
King. Go, call before me all the lords in court.
    Sit, my preserver, by thy patient's side:
    And with this healthful hand, whose banish'd sense 50
    Thou hast repeal'd, a second time receive
    The confirmation of my promis'd gift,
    Which but attends thy naming.

            Enter several Lords.

    Fair maid, send forth thine eye: this youthful parcel
    Of noble bachelors stand at my bestowing, 55
    O'er whom both sovereign power and father's voice
    I have to use: thy frank election make;
    Thou hast power to choose, and they none to forsake.
Hel. To each of you one fair and virtuous mistress
    Fall, when Love please! marry, to each, but one. 60

---

46. *Mort du vinager*] Ff, *Mort du vinaigre* Usu. Rdg., *Mort du vainqueur* Collier. 59, 60. *mistress Fall*,] Rowe, *Mistris; Fall* Ff.

46. *Mor du vinager*] a meaningless oath. Probably Parolles intended to swear in French. The result is unsatisfactory in every way.

47. *'Fore God*] Cf. 1435, Torr. Portugal, 745. "Fore Sen Jame! What ys the gyantes name." The expression "foregad" is a common one (*New Eng. Dict.*).

50. *healthful*] healthy.

51. *repeal'd*] called back, restored from banishment. Cf. "the banished Bolingbroke repeals himself" (*Richard II.* II. ii. 49).

54. *parcel*] party. Cf. "This parcel of wooers" (*Merchant of Venice*, I. ii. 119).

55. *at my bestowing*] The feudal lord might tender a husband to his female ward in her minority, and if she rejected the proposal she forfeited a sum which the guardian could have obtained from such an alliance. This was afterwards extended to male wards (*Student's Hume*, 1870, p. 132).

57. *frank election*] a legal phrase, which, according to Rushton, occurs in 3 Edward I. (Westminster the First), cap. v.

58. *forsake*] refuse, deny (German, *versagen*). An anonymous writer in *Notes and Queries* (5th S. viii. 182, x. 145) quotes B. R[ich], in Greene's *Newes both from Heaven and Hell* (1593), who introduces a bricklayer "who forsooke to goe into heauen because his wife was there."

60. *marry ... one*] One of the many delightful touches which make Helena so charming a character. She means ... ere is only one Lord to whom she cannot wish a fair and

Laf. I'd give bay Curtal and his furniture,
　　My mouth no more were broken than these boys',
　　And writ as little beard.
King.　　　　　　　　　　Peruse them well:
　　Not one of those but had a noble father.
Hel. Gentlemen,　　　　　　　　　　　　　　65
　　Heaven hath through me restor'd the king to health.
All. We understand it, and thank heaven for you.
Hel. I am a simple maid; and therein wealthiest
　　That I protest I simply am a maid.
　　Please it your majesty, I have done already:　70
　　The blushes in my cheeks thus whisper me,
　　"We blush that thou should'st choose; but, be refus'd,
　　Let the white death sit on thy cheek for ever;
　　We'll ne'er come there again."
King.　　　　　　　　　　Make choice; and, see,
　　Who shuns thy love, shuns all his love in me.　75
Hel. Now, Dian, from thy altar do I fly,
　　And to imperial Love, that god most high,
　　Do my sighs stream. Sirs, will you hear my suit?

65, 66.] Capell's arrangement; prose in Ff.　65.] [She addresses her to a Lord.] Ff.　72. *choose; but, be refused*] Rann; *choose, but be refused* F 1, 2, 3. 77. *imperial Love*] *imperiall loue* F 1; *imperial Joue* F 2; *impartial Joue* F 3, 4. 78. *Sirs*] Thiselton conj., *Sir* Ff.

virtuous mistress, because that one is to have her to wife.
　61. *Curtal*] 1530, Palsgr. 68, *Covrtavlt*, a courtall, a horse. *Ibid.* 506–1. "I wyll cutte of my horse tayle and make hym a courtault" (*New Eng. Dict.*).
　61. *furniture*] trappings. Cf. "The horse's furniture must be of very sensible colours" (Dryden).
　62. *broken*] a broken mouth is one which has lost part of its teeth (Johnson).
　63. *writ as little beard*] Cf. "as if he had writ man since his father was a bachelor" (*2 Henry IV.* 1. ii. 30).
　72. *be refus'd*] In the Ff the semicolon is put after "refused": the punctuation here given has been adopted by most editors, as it makes more sense. "But if you are refused, let your cheeks be for ever pale, for we will never come again." The personification of blushes is as beautiful as it is scarce.
　78. *Sirs*] The Ff read "Sir," as if Helena addressed herself only to one Lord. The context supports Thisel-

First Lord. And grant it.
Hel. Thanks, sir; all the rest is mute.
Laf. I had rather be in this choice than throw 80
  ames-ace for my life.
Hel. The honour, sir, that flames in your fair eyes,
  Before I speak, too threateningly replies:
  Love make your fortunes twenty times above
  Her that so wishes, and her humble love! 85
Second Lord. No better, if you please.
Hel. My wish receive,
  Which great Jove grant! and so I take my
  leave.
Laf. Do all they deny her? An they were sons of
  mine I'd have them whipped, or I would send
  them to the Turk to make eunuchs of. 90
Hel. Be not afraid that I your hand should take;
  I'll never do you wrong for your own sake:
  Blessing upon your vows! and in your bed
  Find fairer fortune, if you ever wed!
Laf. These boys are boys of ice, they'll none have 95
  her: sure, they are bastards to the English; the
  French ne'er got 'em.

80, 81.] Prose in Pope. In the Ff, two verses ending *throw . . . life*.
81. *ames-ace*] F 1; *A deaus-ace* F 2, 3, 4.   87. *Jove*] F 3, 4; *love* F 1, 2.
88. *An*] Capell, *And* Ff.

ton's conjecture, that "the comma after 'Sir' may have been 's' in the MS."
  79. *the rest is mute*] the others are all silent.
  80. *I had rather . . .*] This passage as usually interpreted seems rather foolish. I suspect that Lafeu means he would very much like to be in this choice—"for my life!" may be an exclamation. "Ames-ace" (two sixes of dice) is used in modern English. Lowell (*Shakespeare Once More, Essays on the English Poets,* Walter Scott ed.) writes: " . . . risk the prosperity of a verse upon a lucky throw of words, which may come up the sixes of hardy metaphor or the ambsace of conceit."
  83. *Before I speak*] Helen, passing the second lord, pays him this compliment to excuse her refusal.

Hel. You are too young, too happy, and too good,
    To make yourself a son out of my blood.
Fourth Lord. Fair one, I think not so.   100
Laf. There's one grape yet; I am sure thy father
    drank wine. But if thou be'st not an ass, I am
    a youth of fourteen: I have known thee already.
Hel. [*To Bertram.*] I dare not say I take you; but I give
    Me and my service, ever whilst I live,   105
    Into your guiding power. This is the man.
King. Why, then, young Bertram, take her; she's thy wife.
Ber. My wife, my liege! I shall beseech your highness,
    In such a business give me leave to use
    The help of mine own eyes.
King.   Know'st thou not, Bertram, 110
    What she has done for me?
Ber.   Yes, my good lord;
    But never hope to know why I should marry her.
King. Thou know'st she has rais'd me from my sickly bed.
Ber. But follows it, my lord, to bring me down
    Must answer for your raising? I know her well: 115
    She had her breeding at my father's charge.
    A poor physician's daughter my wife! Disdain
    Rather corrupt me ever!
King. 'Tis only title thou disdain'st in her, the which

101, 102]. Theobald (Warburton) arrange as follows: "Laf. *There's one grape yet,—* Par. *I am sure thy father drank wine.* Laf. *But if . . .*" 104.] [To Bertram.] Rowe. 107. *Why . . . wife*] verse Rowe; prose Ff. 110–113. *Know'st thou . . . bed*] verse Pope; prose Ff.

98. *You are too young . . .*] This speech is, in Ff, attributed to Lafeu.
101, 102. *thy father drank wine*] therefore thou shouldest have fire within thy skin (Delius).
103. *known thee already*] Am sure of it, from what I have seen of you.

117, 118. *Disdain Rather corrupt me ever*] disgrace make me ever despicable in future.
119. *only title*] only lack of title. Cf. "I almost die for food" (*As You Like It*, II. vii. 104).

I can build up. Strange is it that our bloods, 120
Of colour, weight, and heat, pour'd all together,
Would quite confound distinction, yet stands off
In differences so mighty. If she be
All that is virtuous, save what thou dislik'st,
A poor physician's daughter, thou dislik'st 125
Of virtue for the name; but do not so:
From lowest place when virtuous things proceed,
The place is dignified by the doer's deed:
Where great additions swell's, and virtue none,
It is a dropsied honour. Good alone 130
Is good without a name? Vileness is so:
The property by what it is should go,
Not by the title. She is young, wise, fair;
In these to nature she's immediate heir,
And these breed honour: that is honour's scorn 135
Which challenges itself as honour's born,
And is not like the sire: honours thrive

127. *place when*] Theobald (Thirlby conj.), *place, whence* Ff.   129. *additions swell's*] F 1; *addition swell's* F 2; *addition swells* F 3 4; *additions swells* Malone.   130, 131. *Good alone Is good without a name? Vileness is so*] F 1, 2, 3. Most editors follow F 4, which drops the note of interrogation after name.   137. *honours thrive*] F 1; *honours best thrive* F 2, 3, 4.

120. *bloods*] plural form with singular meaning.
121. *Of colour . . . heat*] Either, as Malone understands, "of one and same colour (etc.)," or else "as regards colour (etc.)." The latter is the meaning given by Abbott.
124. *what thou dislik'st*] This seems to refer to "a poor physician's daughter."
125, 126. *dislik'st Of*] Cf. "If you like of me" (*Much Ado*, v. iv. 59).
129. *additions*] "In our common lat. law 'addition' signifieth any title given to a man besides his name" (Bullokar, *An English Expositor*,

quoted by W. J. Craig in his "Little Quarto Shakespeare").
129. *swell's*] probably for "swell us," as Boswell explains.
130, 131. *Good alone . . . name?*] Is only goodness good when it has no title? No, for vileness is vile when it has no title. "Let's write good angel on the devil's horn, 'Tis not the devil's crest" (Steevens).
136. *challenges itself*] makes a claim for itself.
137. *honours thrive*) F 2, 3, 4 read "honours *best* thrive." But "sire" is a dissyllable (Abbott's *Grammar*, 480).

When rather from our acts we them derive,
Than our foregoers: the mere words a slave,
Debosh'd on every tomb, on every grave, 140
A lying trophy, and as oft is dumb
Where dust and damn'd oblivion is the tomb
Of honour'd bones indeed. What should be said?
If thou canst like this creature as a maid,
I can create the rest: virtue and she 145
Is her own dower; honour and wealth from me.

Ber. I cannot love her, nor will strive to do 't.

King. Thou wrong'st thyself if thou should'st strive to
choose.

Hel. That you are well restor'd, my lord, I'm glad:
Let the rest go. 150

King. My honour's at the stake, which to defeat
I must produce my power. Here, take her hand,
Proud scornful boy, unworthy this good gift,
That dost in vile misprision shackle up

---

139. *words*] F 1; *word's* F 2, 3, 4.   140. *grave*] *grave:* Ff.   142, 143. *tomb Of . . . indeed*] Theobald (Thirlby conj.), *Tombe. Of . . . indeed* Ff.
151. *defeat*] *defend* Theobald.

138.] "The pith o' sense and pride o' worth Are higher ranks than a' that."

139. *words*] same construction as in *Coriolanus,* IV. v. 242, "as warres may be said to be *a ravisher.*"

140. *Debosh'd*] vitiated and worthless; now spelled debauched.

143. *honour'd bones*] bones worthy of being honoured.

145. *virtue and she*] Perhaps we should read "virtue—and she is her own dower"; meaning "as far as virtue is concerned she has nothing to receive in addition" (conj. by H. T., author of *Was Shakespeare a Lawyer?*).

148. *strive to choose*] Bertram being the king's ward has no right to choose.

151. *which to defeat*] "which" here refers to the loss of his honour, which the king implies by saying that it is at the stake. Malone quotes the parallel in *Othello,* ". . . She dying gave it me, And bid me, when my fate would have me wive, To give it her," *i.e.* to my wife, though not before mentioned but by implication. Theobald prefers to change "defeat," writing instead "defend."

152. *produce*] unsheath as a sword drawn from its scabbard.

154. *misprision*] "Misprision is included in every treason or felony, and

My love and her desert; that canst not dream, 155
We, poising us in her defective scale,
Shall weigh thee to the beam; that wilt not know,
It is in us to plant thine honour where
We please to have it grow.   Check thy contempt:
Obey our will, which travails in thy good: 160
Believe not thy disdain, but presently
Do thine own fortunes that obedient right
Which both thy duty owes and our power claims;
Or I will throw thee from my care for ever
Into the staggers and the careless lapse 165
Of youth and ignorance; both my revenge and hate
Loosing upon thee, in the name of justice,
Without all terms of pity.   Speak; thine answer.
Ber. Pardon, my gracious lord; for I submit
My fancy to your eyes.   When I consider 170
What great creation and what dole of honour

165. *careless*] *cureless* Dyce (ed. 2), S. Walker conj.

when any one hath committed treason or felony the king may order that he shall be indicted for misprision only" (Wood's *Institutes*, 2nd ed., 406). "The king (here) probably uses it in a double sense, signifying wrong or false imprisonment . . . and also signifying contempt, with which word it is connected with the passage below, III. ii. 31" (Rushton). Cf. *1 Henry IV.* I. iii. 27, and *Twelfth Night*, I. v. 61.

165. *staggers*] Shakespeare uses this word once in its literal sense of a disease in horses, "Spoiled with the staggers" (*Taming of the Shrew*, III. ii. 55). Here it is used to signify a giddy and useless existence. Beaumont and Fletcher write, "Poor Gentleman, he's troubled with the staggers."

165. *careless*] Dyce has a strong case for the emendation "cureless," quoting W. W. Williams (*The Parthenon*, Nov. 1, 1862): "I have always considered 'cureless' to be the author's word. 1. Because 'care' in the one line, and 'careless' in the other, where no verbal resemblance can be intended, presents an anti-Shakespearian cacophony. 2. We have countless misprints of the same kind: as in *Troilus and Cressida*, where the Q gives us 'destruction' and the F 'distraction.' 3. Lapse=fall; and the king is unmistakably warning Bertram that, if he does not obey him, he will let him go his own headstrong way to irreparable ruin. As, 'Repair thy wit, good youth, or it will fall To cureless ruin,' *Merchant of Venice*, IV. i. 141."

171. *dole of honour*] share of honour. See *Henry V.* IV. iii. 22.

     Flies where you bid it, I find that she, which late
     Was in my nobler thoughts most base, is now
     The praised of the king; who, so ennobled,
     Is as 'twere born so.

King.   Take her by the hand,   175
     And tell her she is thine: to whom I promise
     A counterpoise; if not to thy estate,
     A balance more replete.

Ber.   I take her hand.

King. Good fortune and the favour of the king
     Smile upon this contract; whose ceremony   180
     Shall seem expedient on the now-born brief,
     And be perform'd to-night: the solemn feast
     Shall more attend upon the coming space,
     Expecting absent friends. As thou lov'st her,

---

172. *bid it*] *bid* Rowe.   179. *king*] S. Walker conj. a corruption.   181. *now-born*] *now borne* F 1, 2; *now born* F 3, 4; *new-born* Warburton.

177. *if not . . . estate*] if she be not thine equal in rank, I will make the balance more replete. Cf. "fortune now to my heart's hope!" (*Merchant of Venice*, II. ix. 20); "to her own worth she shall be prized" (*Troilus and Cressida*, IV. iv. 135); "a soldier even to Cato's wish" (*Coriolanus*, I. iv. 57).

179. *king*] S. Walker conjectures that this word is a misprint, being a repetition of the same word which occurs a few lines above. It does seem curious that the king should thus speak of himself twice running. Perhaps it should be "the favour of the Lord."

181. *seem . . . brief*] "seem" here means figure or be notified as expedient . . . be found to be expedient. "Now-born" means either just written or now borne away; it is difficult to say which. Does brief mean a letter? If so, is it the letter despatched by the Countess to Helena (II. ii. 66) of which the king may have heard during his conversation with Bertram? (Schmidt). Is it a summary or temporary contract as in "She told me in a sweet verbal brief" (which occurs below, v. iii. 137)? Or is it something that will be developed afterwards? "The hand of time shall draw this brief into as huge a volume." (*King John*, II. 103). Or does it mean "a royal command"? There is no deciding, I think.

183. *Shall . . . space*] another obscure phrase. Probably means "shall not take place in the immediate future, at all events until the expected absent friends arrive." This passage seems obscurely to prophesy that the feast would be postponed, and that it would eventually be a matter of expecting absent friends—only the audience know what friends.

Thy love's to me religious; else, does err.   185
        [*Exeunt. Parolles and Lafeu stay behind,*
        commenting of this wedding.

Laf. Do you hear, monsieur? a word with you.
Par. Your pleasure, sir.
Laf. Your lord and master did well to make his recantation.
Par. Recantation! My lord! my master!   190
Laf. Ay; is it not a language I speak?
Par. A most harsh one, and not to be understood without bloody succeeding. My master!
Laf. Are you companion to the Count Rousillon?
Par. To any count; to all counts; to what is man.   195
Laf. To what is count's man: count's master is of another style.
Par. You are too old, sir; let it satisfy you, you are too old.
Laf. I must tell thee, sirrah, I write man; to which   200
title age cannot bring thee.
Par. What I dare too well do, I dare not do.
Laf. I did think thee, for two ordinaries, to be a pretty wise fellow: thou didst make tolerable vent of thy travel; it might pass: yet the scarfs and the   205
bannerets about thee did manifoldly dissuade me

203. *ordinaries, to*] *ordinaries: to* F 1, 2; *ordinaries to* F 3, 4.

193. *bloody succeeding*] subsequent shedding of blood.
195. *to what is man*] Parolles doubtless means to imply that Lafeu is no man. Lafeu takes the word in another sense.
200. *I write man*] Cf. "Albeit I did write man, yet I was but a young lad . . . and a meere child in the knowledge of these things" (Mabbe's translation of *Guzman de Alfarache*, 1623, W. G. Stone, *New Sh. Soc. Trans.*, 1880–85, p. 399).
203. *two ordinaries*] two meals, two days. Cf. "goes to the feast and for his ordinary pays his heart for what his eyes eat only" (*Antony and Cleopatra*, II. ii. 230).

from believing thee a vessel of too great a burthen.
I have now found thee; when I lose thee again,
I care not; yet art thou good for nothing but
taking up, and that thou'rt scarce worth. 210

Par. Hadst thou not the privilege of antiquity upon
thee,—

Laf. Do not plunge thyself too far in anger, lest thou
hasten thy trial; which if—Lord have mercy on
thee for a hen! So, my good window of lattice, 215
fare thee well: thy casement I need not open, for
I look through thee. Give me thy hand.

Par. My lord, you give me most egregious indignity.

Laf. Ay, with all my heart; and thou art worthy
of it. 220

Par. I have not, my lord, deserved it.

Laf. Yes, good faith, every dram of it; and I will not
bate thee a scruple.

Par. Well, I shall be wiser—

Laf. E'en as soon as thou canst, for thou hast to pull 225
at a smack o' the contrary. If ever thou be'st
bound in thy scarf and beaten, thou shalt find
what it is to be proud of thy bondage. I have
a desire to hold my acquaintance with thee, or

---

214. *if—*] Theobald; *if*, F 1, 2; *is*, F 3, 4.   224. *wiser—*] Theobald, *wiser.*
Ff.   225, 226. *thou hast to pull at a smack o' the contrary*] *thou hast too full a smack* Daniel conj.

210. *taking up*] Johnson says that "to take up" is to contradict, to call to account. Cf. the quibble "take this shadow up, for 'tis thy rival" (*Two Gentlemen of Verona*, IV. iv. 202); "a whoreson jackanapes must take me up for swearing" (*Cymbeline*, II. i. 4).

215. *a hen*] term of contempt, as in "hen-hearted."

215. *lattice*] ale-house window.

225, 226. *pull at . . . contrary*] pull or draw at a taste of folly, as at a vessel: taste or considerable amount. Schmidt asks "with a pun? meaning also a small vessel, a sloop?" Cf. "some smack of age" (*2 Henry IV.* I. ii. 111).

rather my knowledge, that I may say in the 230
default, he is a man I know.
Par. My lord, you do me most insupportable
vexation.
Laf. I would it were hell-pains for thy sake, and my
poor doing eternal: for doing I am past; as I will 235
by thee, in what motion age will give me leave.
[*Exit.*
Par. Well, thou hast a son shall take this disgrace
off me; scurvy, old, filthy, scurvy lord! Well, I
must be patient; there is no fettering of authority.
I'll beat him, by my life, if I can meet him with 240
any convenience, an he were double and double
a lord. I'll have no more pity of his age than I
would have of—I'll beat him, an if I could but
meet him again!

Re-enter LAFEU.

Laf. Sirrah, your lord and master's married; there's 245
news for you: you have a new mistress.
Par. I most unfeignedly beseech your lordship to
make some reservation of your wrongs: he is my
good lord: whom I serve above is my master.
Laf. Who? God? 250

235, 236.] Probably corrupt. Hanmer considers "for doing . . . leave" spurious. Warburton supposes a line to be lost after "past." 250. *God?*] F 4; *God.* F 1, 2, 3.

230, 231. *in the default*] when necessary, needful.
236. *by thee*] Malone explains this as a conceit. "I am past: but I will pass by thee . . ."

248, 249. *he is . . . master*] a strange construction: but the emendations of Rowe and Pope involve the omission of "is," and seem rather bold.

Par. Ay, sir.

Laf. The devil it is that's thy master. Why dost thou garter up thy arms o' this fashion? dost make hose of thy sleeves? do other servants so? Thou wert best set thy lower part where thy nose 255 stands. By mine honour, if I were but two hours younger, I'd beat thee: methinks 't thou art a general offence, and every man should beat thee: I think thou wast created for men to breathe themselves upon thee. 260

Par. This is hard and undeserved measure, my lord.

Laf. Go to, sir; you were beaten in Italy for picking a kernel out of a pomegranate; you are a vagabond and no true traveller: you are more saucy with lords and honourable personages than the 265 commission of your birth and virtue gives you heraldry. You are not worth another word, else I'd call you knave. I leave you. [*Exit.*

Par. Good, very good; it is so then: good, very good; let it be concealed awhile. 270

---

253. *o'*] Rowe (ed. 2), *a* Ff.   257. *methinks 't*] Dyce (S. Walker conj.), *methink'st* Ff.

254. *make hose of thy sleeves*] Halliwell cites Fairholt to show how servants used to gather up their long sleeves and tuck them into their girdles in order that those fashionable appendages might not be in the way while they were attending to their duties. (Ladies who wear fashionable sleeves will understand.)

257. *methinks 't*] it thinks or seems to me. Cf. "Thinks 't thee" in *Hamlet*.

259, 260. *breathe themselves upon*] as an exercise for them.

263. *pomegranate*] Rushton suggests that this may mean "that Parolles was punished for sending a letter in a pomegranate, like Euphues's Philautus, who "at the last taking out of his closette a fayre Pomegranat and pullying all the Kernelles out of it, hee wrapped his Letter in it."

267. *heraldry*] rank or the right of rank. Cleveland uses the word in much the same sense when he says "she makes pearls and planets humble heraldry." Hanmer would read "the heraldry of your birth and virtue gives you commission.'

Re-enter BERTRAM.

Ber. Undone, and forfeited to cares for ever!
Par. What's the matter, sweet heart?
Ber. Although before the solemn priest I have sworn, I
    will not bed her.
Par. What, what, sweet heart? 275
Ber. O my Parolles, they have married me!
    I'll to the Tuscan wars, and never bed her.
Par. France is a dog-hole, and it no more merits
    The tread of a man's foot. To the wars!
Ber. There's letters from my mother: what the im- 280
    port is, I know not yet.
Par. Ay, that would be known. To the wars, my boy!
    to the wars!
    He wears his honour in a box, unseen,
    That hugs his kicky-wicky here at home,
    Spending his manly marrow in her arms, 285
    Which should sustain the bound and high curvet
    Of Mars's fiery steed. To other regions!
    France is a stable; we that dwell in 't jades;
    Therefore, to the war!
Ber. It shall be so: I'll send her to my house, 290
    Acquaint my mother with my hate to her,

---

270. Re-enter Bertram] Dyce; Enter Count Rossillion Ff (after line 268).
284. *kicky-wicky*] *kickie-wickie* F 1; *kicksie-wicksie* F 2, 3. 287, 288. *regions!*
France] Capell, *regions, France* Ff.

280. *letters*] a letter, as in Latin.
286. *curvet*] "Amongst these salts and leaps the corvette, or curvet, was highly esteemed." It was "a certaine continuall pransing and dansing up and downe still in one place, like a beare at a stake and sometimes sideling to and fro, wherein the horse maketh as though he would fain run and cannot be suffered" (D. H. Madden quoting Gervase Markham).

And wherefore I am fled; write to the king
That which I durst not speak: his present-gift
Shall furnish me to those Italian fields,
Where noble fellows strike. Wars is no strife   295
To the dark house and the detested wife.
Par. Will this capriccio hold in thee? art sure?
Ber. Go with me to my chamber, and advise me.
I'll send her straight away: to-morrow
I'll to the wars, she to her single sorrow.   300
Par. Why, these balls bound; there's noise in it. 'Tis hard:
A young man married is a man that's marr'd:
Therefore away, and leave her bravely; go:
The king has done you wrong: but, hush! 'tis so.
[*Exeunt.*

SCENE IV.—*Another Room in the Same.*

Enter HELENA *and Clown.*

Hel. My mother greets me kindly: is she well?
Clo. She is not well; but yet she has her health: she's very merry; but yet she is not well: but

---

296. *detested*] Rowe, *detected* Ff. *betimes to-morrow* Steevens conj. Delius.
299. *to-morrow*] *even to-morrow* Hanmer,
303. *her bravely; go:*] *her; bravely go:*

294. *furnish me to*] equip with what is necessary for. "To furnish thee to Belmont"(*Merchant of Venice*, I. i. 182).
296. *detested*] In the margin of the third Folio belonging to the Capell collection an unknown hand has made the correction "detested" for "detected" (Cambridge Editors).
299. *to-morrow*] perhaps we should read "and to-morrow." There is evidently something missing.
301. *balls bound*] meaning that just as when balls bound with a noise they are as they should be, so are Bertram's words. Proverbial.
302. *married . . . marr'd*] a trite joke. Cf. *Merry Wives*, I. i. 25, "*Shallow.* You may by marrying. *Evans.* It is marring indeed." Rushton quotes Puttenham as giving "The maide that soone married is, soone marred." *Marrying marring* is one of the proverbs of J. H. Sharman, p. 144 (W. J. C.).

thanks be given, she's very well, and wants
nothing i' the world; but yet she is not well. 5
Hel. If she be very well, what does she ail, that she's
not very well?
Clo. Truly, she's very well indeed, but for two
things.
Hel. What two things? 10
Clo. One, that she's not in heaven, whither God send
her quickly! the other, that she's in earth, from
whence God send her quickly!

Enter PAROLLES.

Par. Bless you, my fortunate lady!
Hel. I hope, sir, I have your good will to have mine 15
own good fortunes.
Par. You had my prayers to lead them on; and to
keep them on, have them still. O! my knave,
how does my old lady?
Clo. So that you had her wrinkles, and I her money, 20
I would she did as you say.
Par. Why, I say nothing.
Clo. Marry, you are the wiser man; for many a man's
tongue shakes out his master's undoing. To say
nothing, to do nothing, to know nothing, and to 25
have nothing, is to be a great part of your title;
which is within a very little of nothing.

11. *whither*] *whether* F 1. 16. *fortunes*] Capell (Heath conj.), *fortune* Ff (the following "them" requires a plural noun, but it is by no means certain that Shakespeare used one).

24. *shakes out*] a similar metaphor occurs in the Bible. "Also I shook my lap, and said, So God shake out every man from his house, and from his labour . . . even thus be he shaken out, and emptied" (Neh. v. 13). 26. *your title*] Title is here used meaning "one's intrinsic value."

Par. Away! th' art a knave.

Clo. You should have said, sir, before a knave th' art
a knave; that's, before me th'rt a knave: this 30
had been truth, sir.

Par. Go to, thou art a witty fool; I have found thee.

Clo. Did you find me in yourself, sir, or were you
taught to find me?

Par. * * * 35

Clo. The search, sir, was profitable; and much fool
may you find in you, even to the world's pleasure
and the increase of laughter.

Par. A good knave, i' faith, and well fed.
Madam, my lord will go away to-night; 40
A very serious business calls on him.
The great prerogative and rite of love,
Which, as your due, time claims, he does acknowledge,
But puts it off to a compell'd restraint;
Whose want, and whose delay, is strew'd with
sweets, 45
Which they distil now in the curbed time,

34.] There can be little doubt that a speech of Parolles has been lost here. Probably (as several editors have conjectured) something equivalent to "in myself." 44. *to*] F 1, 2; *by* F 3, 4. 46. *curbed time*] Ff, *cup of time* Collier conj.

28, 29. *th' art*] old way of apostrophising "thou art."

32. *found thee*] Cf. "I have found you, your lays and out-leaps, Junius" (Beaumont and Fletcher, *Bonduca*, I. iii.).

36. *The search, sir ...*] This passage is as it were a separate speech in the Ff; though the foregoing sentence is also given to the clown. Perhaps some remark is missing between "find me" and "the search." Parolles may have said something in which the word "search" occurred.

Collier supplies the missing speech from the MS. notes, namely, "*Par.* Go to, I say: I have found thee: no more; I have found thee, a witty fool."

39. *well fed*] Ritson suggests that this is an allusion to the old saying, "Better fed than taught," to which the clown has himself alluded in a preceding scene: "I will show myself highly fed and lowly taught."

46. *curbed time*] Collier suggested "cup of time," a very beautiful emendation, so plausible as to be almost convincing.

To make the coming hour o'erflow with joy,
And pleasure drown the brim.

Hel. What's his will else?

Par. That you will take your instant leave o' the king,
And make this haste as your own good proceeding, 50
Strengthen'd with what apology you think
May make it probable need.

Hel. What more commands he?

Par. That, having this obtain'd, you presently
Attend his further pleasure.

Hel. In every thing I wait upon his will. 55

Par. I shall report it so. [*Exit Parolles.*

Hel. [*To Clown.*] I pray you come, sirrah. [*Exeunt.*

SCENE V.—*Another Room in the Same.*

Enter LAFEU *and* BERTRAM.

Laf. But I hope your lordship thinks not him a soldier.

Ber. Yes, my lord, and of very valiant approof.

Laf. You have it from his own deliverance.

Ber. And by other warranted testimony. 5

Laf. Then my dial goes not true: I took this lark for a bunting.

---

52. *need*] omitted Gould conj.

48. *drown the brim*] an expression often used to signify overflow, as when rivers "drown their shores."

52. *probable need*] a likely or plausible necessity.

53. *this*] refers to taking leave of the king, and the leave he was to give.

Scene V.

3. *valiant approof*] approved valour (see above, I. ii. 50).

4. *deliverance*] speech, as elsewhere in Shakespeare.

6. *took this lark . . .*] "The bunting is, in feather, size, and form, so like

Ber. I do assure you, my lord, he is very great in
    knowledge, and accordingly valiant.
Laf. I have then sinned against his experience and   10
    transgressed against his valour; and my state
    that way is dangerous, since I cannot yet find
    in my heart to repent. Here he comes; I pray
    you, make us friends; I will pursue the amity.

               Enter PAROLLES.

Par. [*To Bertram.*] These things shall be done, sir.   15
Laf. Pray you, sir, who's his tailor?
Par. Sir?
Laf. O! I know him well. Ay, sir; he, sir, 's a good
    workman, a very good tailor.
Ber. [*Aside to Parolles.*] Is she gone to the king?   20
Par. She is.
Ber. Will she away to-night?
Par. As you'll have her.
Ber. I have writ my letters, casketed my treasure,
    given order for our horses; and to-night, when   25
    I should take possession of the bride, end ere I
    do begin.

---

15. [To Bertram] Capell, omitted Ff.   18. *Ay*] Capell, *I* Ff. *sir,'s*] Theobald; *sirs* F 1; *sir's* F 2, 3, 4.   20. [Aside to Parolles] Rowe, omitted Ff. 24-27.] Arrangement as in Pope; verse Ff.   26. *end*] Collier, *and* Ff.

the skylark, as to require nice attention to discover the one from the other; it also ascends and sinks in the air nearly in the same manner; but it has little or no song, which gives estimation to the skylark" (Johnson). Barrett's *Alvearie*, 1580, gives it as "*avis alaudae similis*. . . ." Bunting and lark are frequently found together in old ballads and nursery rhymes.

9. *accordingly*] in proportion to his very great knowledge.
16. *his tailor*] your tailor.
26, 27. *end . . . begin*] The emendation "end" for "and" was made by someone in Lord Ellesmere's copy of the Folio. Cf. "You always end ere you begin" (*Two Gentlemen of Verona*, II. iv. 31).

Laf. A good traveller is something at the latter end
of a dinner; but one that lies three thirds, and
uses a known truth to pass a thousand nothings 30
with, should be once heard and thrice beaten.
God save you, captain.
Ber. Is there any unkindness between my lord and
you, monsieur?
Par. I know not how I have deserved to run into my 35
lord's displeasure.
Laf. You have made shift to run into 't, boots and
spurs and all, like him that leaped into the
custard; and out of it you'll run again, rather
than suffer question for your residence. 40
Ber. It may be you have mistaken him, my lord.
Laf. And shall do so ever, though I took him at 's
prayers. Fare you well, my lord; and believe
this of me, there can be no kernel in this light
nut; the soul of this man is his clothes. Trust 45
him not in matter of heavy consequence; I have
kept of them tame, and know their natures.
Farewell, monsieur: I have spoken better of you
than you have or will to deserve at my hand;
but we must do good against evil. [*Exit.* 50
Par. An idle lord, I swear.

29. *one*] Rowe (ed. 2), *on* Ff.   31. *heard*] *hard* F 1.   49. *have or will*] *your 'haviour wills* Bulloch (conj.), *have qualities or will* Malone (conj.), *wit or will* Singer (conj.), *power or will* Lettsom (conj.).

28. *good traveller*] Lafeu harps upon Parolles' boasted travels.
39. *custard*] Theobald says that "It was a foolery practised at city entertainments, whilst the jester ... was in vogue, for him to jump into a large deep custard, set for the purpose...."
Ben Jonson alludes to the practice in *Devil's an Ass*, I. i.
47. *kept ... tame*] I have kept some such creatures tame.
51. *idle*] silly. Cf. "And their words seemed to them as idle tales, and they believed them not" (S. Luke

Ber. I think not so.
Par. Why, do you know him?
Ber. Yes, I do know him well; and common speech
    Gives him a worthy pass. Here comes my clog. 55

Enter HELENA.

Hel. I have, sir, as I was commanded from you,
    Spoke with the king, and have procur'd his leave
    For present parting; only he desires
    Some private speech with you.
Ber.   I shall obey his will.
You must not marvel, Helen, at my course,   60
    Which holds not colour with the time, nor does
    The ministration and required office
    On my particular: prepar'd I was not
    For such a business; therefore am I found
    So much unsettled. This drives me to entreat you, 65
    That presently you take your way for home;
    And rather muse than ask why I entreat you;

---

52. *not*] S. Walker (conj.) and Singer (ed. 2), omitted Ff.   53. *know him?*] S. Walker (conj.) and Singer (ed. 2), *not know him* Ff.

xxiv. 11). See also IV. iii. 219, below.
52, 53.] The Ff read "*Ber.* I think so. *Par.* Why, do you not know him?" That seems to be wrong. The "not" must have been put in the wrong place. Delius takes "I think so" to be a modification of "I swear." If so the original might stand—but it seems rather a far-fetched meaning.
63. *On my particular*] as far as I am concerned. Cf. *Antony and Cleopatra*, IV. ix. 20, "Forgive me in thine own particular." Also *ibid.*, I. iii. 54, "My more particular is Fulvia's death."

67. *muse*] wonder. "Do not muse at me, my worthy friends" (*Macbeth*, III. iv. 85). "I muse your majesty doth seem so cold" (*King John*, III. i. 317). Milton (*Paradise Lost*, vii. 52) has "filled With admiration and deep muse"; also vi. 581, "while we suspense Collected stood within our thoughts amused."
67. *entreat you*] This is probably another misprint. The expression "entreat you" occurs just above, and there can be little doubt that Shakespeare must have used some other words in the second case. S. Walker suggests the reading "dismiss you."

        For my respects are better than they seem,
        And my appointments have in them a need
        Greater than shows itself at the first view   70
        To you that know them not. This to my mother.
                                    [*Giving a letter.*
        'Twill be two days ere I shall see you, so
        I leave you to your wisdom.
Hel.   Sir, I can nothing say, but that I am
        Your most obedient servant.
Ber. Come, come, no more of that.
Hel.   And ever shall   75
        With true observance seek to eke out that
        Wherein toward me my homely stars have fail'd
        To equal my great fortune.
Ber.   Let that go:
        My haste is very great. Farewell: hie home.
Hel. Pray sir, your pardon.
Ber.   Well, what would you say? 80
Hel. I am not worthy of the wealth I owe,
        Nor dare I say 'tis mine, and yet it is;
        But, like a timorous thief, most fain would steal
        What law does vouch mine own.
Ber.   What would you have?
Hel. Something, and scarce so much: nothing, indeed. 85

---

71. [Giving a letter] Rowe, omitted Ff.   73, 74.] Arranged according to S. Walker's conj.; in Ff two lines, the first ending with "say."   78, 79.] Arranged as in Pope; F 1, 2, 3 read two lines ending "farewell . . . home"; F 4 is prose.

68. *respects*] reasons. Cf. "This argues conscience in your grace, but the respects thereof are nice and trivial" (*Richard III.* III. vii. 175). Also "When such profound respects do pull you on" (*King John,* III. i. 318).

81. *owe*] possess. (See III, ii. 124, below; and II. i. 9, above.)

I would not tell you what I would, my lord:—
Faith, yes;
Strangers and foes do sunder, and not kiss.
Ber. I pray you, stay not, but in haste to horse.
Hel. I shall not break your bidding, good my lord. 90
Ber. Where are my other men, monsieur? Farewell.
                                      [*Exit Helena.*
Go thou toward home; where I will never come
Whilst I can shake my sword or hear the drum.
Away! and for our flight.
Par.   Bravely, coragio!
                                          [*Exeunt.*

ACT III

SCENE I.—*Florence. A Room in the Duke's Palace.*

Flourish. Enter the DUKE OF FLORENCE, *the two Frenchmen, with a troop of Soldiers.*

Duke. So that from point to point now have you heard
The fundamental reasons of this war,

86, 87.] Arranged according to Dyce's conj.; all in one line in the Ff; Hanmer leaves out "my lord."   91. *Where . . . Farewell*] In the Folios the speech is a continuation of Helen's preceding one; emendation by Theobald; *men, monsieur?*] Theobald, *men? Monsieur:* Ff.

91. *Where . . . men*] The Ff give this to Helena. The words may belong to Bertram as Theobald suggested, but as White explains, Helena also must have had a retinue of some sort, and the speech is not nonsense in her mouth. The question is, which of the two is the more likely one to have uttered them? The majority of editors are of the opinion that it is best to give the sentence to Bertram.

  Whose great decision hath much blood let forth
  And more thirsts after.
First Lord.   Holy seems the quarrel
  Upon your Grace's part; black and fearful   5
  On the opposer.
Duke. Therefore we marvel much our cousin France
  Would in so just a business shut his bosom
  Against our borrowing prayers.
Second Lord.   Good my lord,
  The reasons of our state I cannot yield,   10
  But like a common and an outward man,
  That the great figure of a council frames
  By self-unable motion: therefore dare not
  Say what I think of it, since I have found
  Myself in my incertain grounds to fail   15
  As often as I guess'd.
Duke.   Be it his pleasure.
First Lord. But I am sure the younger of our nature,

3. *decision*] action of deciding a contest. Cf. 1538, Starkey, *England*, II. ii. 192, "Thys causyth sutys to be long in decysyon" (*New Eng. Dict.*).

5. *part*] a dissyllable (see Abbott, § 485).

6. *opposer*] the people of Siena. The same construction occurs in *Coriolanus*, I. vi. 27, "More than I know the sound of Marcius' tongue from every meaner man."

9. *Good my lord*] The meaning of the passage is: "Since I can only speak of the reasons of our state as a common and an outward man who conjectures by poor guesses what the council is about, I dare not give an opinion; for I have never been able to make a correct guess yet." The reading of the Ff. may be corrupt—a line or two may be missing.

10. *yield*] communicate.

11. *But like*] except in the capacity of.

11. *outward*] the opposite of the phrase "inward," which occurs in *Measure for Measure*, III. ii. 138, "I was an inward of his."

13. *self-unable motion*] by the unable (weak) motion (conception) of his own self (or brains).

17. *nature*] Rowe changes this to "nation." But I think the word "nature" here means "birth" or "rank." In *2 Henry IV.* I. i. 61, "this man's brow foretells the nature of a tragic volume," the word "nature" seems to have a distinct trace of the original meaning of the word. Again, in *Troilus and Cressida*, V. i. 39, Shakespeare speaks of "diminutives of nature" = by birth.

That surfeit on their ease, will day by day
Come here for physic.
Duke. Welcome they shall be,
And all the honours that can fly from us   20
Shall on them settle. You know your places well;
When better fall, for your avails they fell.
To-morrow to the field.   [*Flourish. Exeunt.*

SCENE II.—*Rousillon. A Room in the Countess's
Palace.*

Enter COUNTESS *and* CLOWN.

Count. It hath happened all as I would have had it,
save that he comes not along with her.
Clo. By my troth, I take my young lord to be a very
melancholy man.
Count. By what observance, I pray you?   5
Clo. Why, he will look upon his boot and sing; mend
the ruff and sing; ask questions and sing; pick his
teeth and sing. I know a man that had this trick
of melancholy sold a goodly manor for a song.

9. *sold*] F 3, 4; *hold* F 1, 2.

22. *When better fall*] Rolfe says, by "better" is meant "your superiors in office": adding that it speaks of places, but means those who fill the places. It may mean, "when better places happen to fall vacant or fall to your share." Cf. *Macbeth*, I. ii. 58, "The victory fell on us"; and *King Lear*, IV. v. 38, "Preferment falls on him that cuts him off."

Scene II.
6, 7. *mend the ruff*] As he speaks of "the" ruff and not of "his" ruff, editors have conjectured that he refers to the ruffles of his boots. According to Fairholt, the fashion of wearing these "ruffs" was introduced into England in the latter part of the sixteenth century.

9. *sold*] The emphasis is clearly on "for a song." The emendation "sold" (first made in F 3) has been almost universally accepted, but "hold" would do if we changed "know" to "knew." "I knew a man hold a

Count. Let me see what he writes, and when he means 10
to come. [*Reads the letter.*]
Clo. I have no mind to Isbel since I was at court.
Our [codlings] and our Isbels o' the country are
nothing like your [codlings] and your Isbels o' the
court: the brains of my Cupid's knocked out, 15
and I begin to love, as an old man loves money,
with no stomach.
Count. What have we here?
Clo. E'en that you have there. [*Exit.*
Count. I have sent you a daughter-in-law: she hath 20
recovered the king, and undone me. I have wedded
her, not bedded her; and sworn to make the "not"
eternal. You shall hear I am run away: know it
before the report come. If there be breadth enough

---

11. [Reads the letter] Theobald, omitted Ff.   13. *codlings*] Kinnear conj.;
old lings F 1; *old ling* F 2, 3, 4.   19. *E'en*] Theobald, *In* Ff.

manor for a song" is much the same as "I never knew a man hold vile stuff so dear" (*Love's Labour's Lost*). Perhaps "hold" means "wager": but I cannot remember an instance of the word "hold" in this sense followed by "for."

9. *manor*] Perhaps any kind of fortune. Cf. *Henry VIII.* I. i. 83, "O many Have broke their backs with laying manors on them For this great journey." Also, Burton's *Anatomy of Melancholy*, Part iii. sec. 2, Mem. iii. subs. 3, "'Tis an ordinary thing to put a thousand oaks and an hundred oxen into a suit of apparel, to wear a whole manor on his back."

13, 14. [*codlings*] Mr. Joseph Crosby wrote to Dr. Herford: "In the county of Westmoreland the peasantry have a very common word to coddle . . . If John is courting Isbel he is said to be coddling her . . . and Isbel is John's coddling." The *New Eng.* *Dict.* says the word "codling" (quodlinge) is used figuratively applied to a raw youth. Ben Jonson, *Alchemist* (ed. Hart), I. i. 189, "*Sub.* Who is it, Dol? *Dol.* A fine young quodling. *Fac.* O, my lawyer's clarke, I lighted on last night." 1640, Shirley, *Captain Underwit*, IV. ii. (In Bullen, *Old Plays*, 1883, ii. 379), "Take a very fine young Codling heire and pound him as small as you can . . . then you must cozen him." 1663, Flagellum; or O. Cromwell, "All the codlings and embryons of Triploe." The Ff read "old ling" or "old lings"—almost certainly a misprint; if not it must mean "the fish," more particularly the lenten fare. "When harvest is ended take shipping or ride, Ling, salt fish and herring for Lent to provide" (Tusser).

15. *the brains of my Cupid's knocked out*] For the plural "brains" with a singular verb, cf. *Hamlet*, III. i. 182; *King Lear*, I. v. 8.

in the world, I will hold a long distance: My duty 25
to you. *Your unfortunate son,*
BERTRAM.

This is not well, rash and unbridled boy,
To fly the favours of so good a king;
To pluck his indignation on thy head 30
By the misprising of a maid too virtuous
For the contempt of empire.

Re-enter Clown.

Clo. O madam! yonder is heavy news within between
two soldiers and my young lady.
Count. What is the matter? 35
Clo. Nay, there is some comfort in the news, some
comfort; your son will not be killed so soon as I
thought he would.
Count. Why should he be killed?
Clo. So say I, madam, if he run away, as I hear he 40
does: the danger is in standing to 't; that's the
loss of men, though it be the getting of children.
Here they come will tell you more; for my part,
I only hear your son was run away. *[Exit.*

Enter HELENA *and two Gentlemen.*

First Gent. Save you, good madam. 45
Hel. Madam, my lord is gone, for ever gone.
Second Gent. Do not say so.

35. *matter?*] F 3, 4; *matter.* F 1, 2.

31. *misprising*] "misprisio (says contempt... and so *mesprise* is ill
Coke) cometh of the word mes-pris, apprehended or known" (Rushton).
which properly signifieth neglect or

Count. Think upon patience. Pray you, gentlemen,
   I have felt so many quirks of joy and grief,
   That the first face of neither, on the start,   50
   Can woman me unto 't: where is my son, I pray you?
Second Gent. Madam, he's gone to serve the Duke of
    Florence:
   We met him thitherward; for thence we came,
   And after some dispatch in hand at court,
   Thither we bend again.   55
Hel. Look on his letter, madam; here's my passport.
   When thou canst get the ring upon my finger,
   which never shall come off, and show me a child
   begotten of thy body that I am father to, then call me
   husband: but in such a "then" I write a "never."   60
   This is a dreadful sentence.
Count. Brought you this letter, gentlemen?
First Gent. Ay, madam; and for the contents' sake
   are sorry for our pains.
Count. I prithee, lady, have a better cheer;   65

---

51. *I pray you?*] omitted Theobald.

51. *Can woman me unto't*] Schmidt points out that as the speaker is a woman the words "unto 't" also must be emphatic. He takes it to mean subdued *like* a woman *to her husband*. Johnson explains, "make pliant as a woman"; Steevens, "it affects me suddenly and deeply."

53. *met him thitherward*] on his way thither.

56. *passport*] anything which gives one free passage to anything. Cf. "A passport to her affection" (Sidney). "The Gospel has then only free admission into the assent of the understanding when it brings a passport from a rightly disposed will" (South). "His passport is his innocence and grace" (Dryden). "Fortune for a passport gave him wealth" (Harte).

57. *get*] take off. Hanmer suggests reading "from my finger." But Shakespeare probably had in mind the passage in Boccaccio's *Giletta of Narbona*—"for I doe purpose to dwell with her, when she shall have this ring (meanyng a ring which he wore) upon her finger . . ."

65. *cheer*] literally face. As in *Midsummer Night's Dream*, III. ii. 96, "all fancy-sick she is and pale of cheer." To "have a better cheer" means to look more cheerful (W. J. C.).

If thou engrossest all the griefs are thine,
Thou robb'st me of a moiety: he was my son,
But I do wash his name out of my blood,
And thou art all my child. Towards Florence is he?
Second Gent. Ay, madam.
Count. And to be a soldier? 70
Second Gent. Such is his noble purpose; and, believe't,
The duke will lay upon him all the honour
That good convenience claims.
Count. Return you thither?
First Gent. Ay, madam, with the swiftest wing of speed.
Hel. [*Reading.*] *Till I have no wife, I have nothing in* 75
France.
'Tis bitter.
Count. Find you that there?
Hel. Ay, madam.
First Gent. 'Tis but the boldness of his hand, haply,
which his heart was not consenting to. 80
Count. Nothing in France, until he have no wife!
There's nothing here that is too good for him
But only she; and she deserves a lord
That twenty such rude boys might tend upon,
And call her hourly mistress. Who was with him? 85
First Gent. A servant only, and a gentleman which I
have sometime known.
Count. Parolles, was it not?

66. *engrossest . . . are*] *all the griefs as thine* Rowe, *these griefs as* (Lettsom conj.). 70. *soldier?*] Pope; Ff have full stop or note of exclamation. 75. [*Reading*] Rowe, omitted Ff.

66. *If thou engrossest*] Steevens paraphrases the line, "If thou keepest all thy sorrows to thyself." Cf. our use of the word in "engrossing" thoughts, desires, etc.

First Gent. Ay, my good lady, he.
Count. A very tainted fellow, and full of wickedness. 90
    My son corrupts a well-derived nature with his
    inducement.
First Gent. Indeed, good lady, the fellow has a deal
    of that too much, which holds him much to
    have. 95
Count. Y' are welcome, gentlemen.
    I will entreat you, when you see my son,
    To tell him that his sword can never win
    The honour that he loses: more I'll entreat you
    Written to bear along.
Second Gent.   We serve you, madam, 100
    In that and all your worthiest affairs.
Count. Not so, but as we change our courtesies.
    Will you draw near?

                    [*Exeunt Countess and Gentlemen.*
Hel. "Till I have no wife, I have nothing in France."
    Nothing in France until he has no wife! 105
    Thou shalt have none, Rousillon, none in France;

---

94. *of that too much*] Rowe, *of that, too much* Ff.

91. *well-derived*] derived, as above (I. i. 45).
91, 92. *with his inducement*] through his influence.
94. *holds him much*] The fellow has a deal of that talent for inducement, which is of so much use to him in his intercourse with Bertram. Cf. 1320, Sir Triste, 918, "What halt it long to striue? Mi leue y take at te." 1380, Sir Ferumb, 1602, "What halt hit much her-of to telle, to drecchen ous of our lay?" (*New Eng. Dict.*).
102. *Not so*] "The Gentlemen declare that they are servants to the Countess; she replies—No otherwise than as she returns the same offices of civility" (Johnson).
104.] Surely Heine misunderstood this passage when he said that Helena's words were not quite honest—that she was playing with words—"no husband in France" meaning one in Italy (etc.)? It seems more likely that Helena did not know where she was going—except that the instinct of love was likely to lead her to the land where Bertram was—for lovers all go the same road whatever their nominal destination may be.

Then hast thou all again. Poor lord! is 't I
That chase thee from thy country, and expose
Those tender limbs of thine to the event
Of the none-sparing war? and is it I 110
That drive thee from the sportive court, where thou
Wast shot at with fair eyes, to be the mark
Of smoky muskets? O you leaden messengers,
That ride upon the violent speed of fire,
Fly with false aim; move the [still-peering] air, 115
That sings with piercing; do not touch my lord!
Whoever shoots at him, I set him there;
Whoever charges on his forward breast,
I am the caitiff that do hold him to 't;
And, though I kill him not, I am the cause 120
His death was so effected: better 'twere
I met the ravin lion when he roar'd
With sharp constraint of hunger; better 'twere
That all the miseries which nature owes

115. [*still-peering*] F 1, *still(-)piercing* F 2, 3, 4; *still-pierced* Nares; *rove the still-piecing* Tyrwhitt; *mow the still-pacing* Jackson conj.; *wound the still-piecing* Collier ed. 2 (Col. MS.); *move the still 'pearing* Delius, 1876; *still closing, still-fleeing, still-fleering, still-recking* (etc.). 116. *sings*] F 1; *stings* F 2, 3, 4. 122. *ravin*] Capell; *ravine* F 1, 2, 3; *raving* F 4.

115. [*still-peering*] This word in the first Folio is probably corrupt; it has, however, been retained in the Cambridge and Globe editions. The editors take it to mean that the air is always ready at hand, however often pierced. The later Ff have still-piercing—an obviously false attempt to better the first Folio. Nares in his Glossary proposes "still pierced," which has the disadvantage of being unlike "still peering." Steevens and Dyce adopt an anonymous conjecture, "still-piecing," which is one of the best emendations. The play on the words "piecing" and "piercing" is quite in keeping with the passage, and "still piecing" gives the idea of the air being pierced without harm. In support of the reading "still 'pearing" Delius quotes *Hamlet*, IV. v. 151, "It shall as level to your judgment peare" (or pierce). Of all the many conjectures, there is no reading, in my opinion, quite as good as Delius's.

122. *the ravin lion*] To ravin is to swallow voraciously; cf. "The ravined salt sea shark" (*Macbeth*, IV. i. 24). The adjective is not elsewhere used by Shakespeare, and is perhaps a corruption of "ravening."

124. *owes*] possesses, as in II. i. 9, and II. v. 81, above.

Were mine at once. No, come thou home, Rousillon,
Whence honour but of danger wins a scar,   126
As oft it loses all: I will be gone;
My being here it is that holds thee hence:
Shall I stay here to do 't? no, no, although
The air of paradise did fan the house,   130
And angels offic'd all: I will be gone,
That pitiful rumour may report my flight,
To consolate thine ear. Come, night; end, day!
For with the dark, poor thief, I'll steal away.
                                              [*Exit.*

SCENE III.—*Florence. Before the Duke's Palace.*

Flourish. Enter DUKE, BERTRAM, PAROLLES, *Soldiers,
        Drum and Trumpets.*

Duke. The general of our horse thou art; and we,
    Great in our hope, lay our best love and credence
    Upon thy promising fortune.
Ber.   Sir, it is
    A charge too heavy for my strength, but yet
    We 'll strive to bear it for your worthy sake   5
    To the extreme edge of hazard.
Duke.   Then go thou forth,
    And fortune play upon thy prosperous helm

---

133. *consolate*] The only instance of the word in Shakespeare. "Console" he does not use at all, and "consolation" only twice. The word consolate is used by other writers, as in Brown's *Vulg. Err.*, "What may somewhat consolate all men that honour virtue, we do not discover the latter scene of his misery in authors of antiquity."

Scene III.

6. *extreme*] accented on the first syllable to correspond to the "utmost" in Milton's imitation, "Ye see our danger on the utmost edge Of hazard."

7. *play upon*] Elsewhere we find Shakespeare speaking of victory playing upon the dancing banners of the French (*King John*, II. i. 307).

As thy auspicious mistress!
Ber. This very day,
Great Mars, I put myself into thy file:
Make me but like my thoughts, and I shall prove   10
A lover of thy drum, hater of love.   [*Exeunt.*

SCENE IV.—*Rousillon. A Room in the Countess's Palace.*

Enter COUNTESS *and Steward.*

Count. Alas! and would you take the letter of her?
Might you not know she would do as she has done,
By sending me a letter? Read it again.
Stew. [*Reads.*] *I am S. Jaques' pilgrim, thither gone:*
Ambitious love hath so in me offended,   5
That bare-foot plod I the cold ground upon
With sainted vow my faults to have amended.
Write, write, that from the bloody course of war,
My dearest master, your dear son, may hie:
Bless him at home in peace, whilst I from far   10
His name with zealous fervour sanctify:

---

3. *letter?*] Pope, *Letter* Ff.   4. [*Reads*] Collier, omitted Ff.   10. peace, whilst] F 3, 4; peace. Whilst F 1, 2.

4. S. Jaques' pilgrim] Commentators have tried to give the shrine some local position. Johnson speaks of S. Jaques de Compostella in Spain, and Reed of Orleans. But Delius thinks it clear that the shrine of S. Jaques must have been in Italy, because Helena passed through Florence on her way to it.
11. His name . . . sanctify] Cf. this line with "But now he's gone, and my idolatrous fancy, Must sanctify his relics" (I. i. 100, above).

    His taken labours bid him me forgive;
    I, his despiteful Juno, sent him forth
    From courtly friends, with camping foes to live,
     Where death and danger dogs the heels of worth:
    He is too good and fair for Death and me;   16
    Whom I myself embrace, to set him free.

Count. Ah! what sharp stings are in her mildest words;
  Rinaldo, you did never lack advice so much,
  As letting her pass so: had I spoke with her,   20
  I could have well diverted her intents,
  Which thus she hath prevented.

Stew.   Pardon me, madam:
  If I had given you this at over-night,
  She might have been o'erta'en; and yet she writes,
  Pursuit would be but vain.

Count.   What angel shall   25
  Bless this unworthy husband? he cannot thrive,
  Unless her prayers, whom heaven delights to hear
  And loves to grant, reprieve him from the wrath
  Of greatest justice. Write, write, Rinaldo,
  To this unworthy husband of his wife;   30

---

  15. dogs] dog Rowe.   18. Count.] Capell, omitted Ff.   19. *Rinaldo*] Rynaldo F 1, 3, 4; *Rynardo* F 2.   26. *husband?*] F 4; husband F 1, 2, 3.   29. *Write, write*] F 1, 3, 4 [pronounce *Writè writè*]; *write and write* F 2.

  12. His taken labours] an indirect reference to the labours of Hercules.

  15. dogs] Several editors change this to "dog." But the singular verb with two subjects occurs frequently. (See Abbott.)

  19. *advice*] forethought or judgment. Cf. "That's not suddenly to be performed, but with advice and silent secrecy" (*2 Henry VI.* II. ii. 68).

  23. *over-night*] Johnson (*Dict.*) says: "This seems to be used by Shakespeare as a noun (meaning night before bedtime), but by Addison more properly as a noun (night) with a preposition (over)." Addison writes: "Will confesses that for half his life his head ached every morning with reading men over night."

Let every word weigh heavy of her worth
That he does weigh too light: my greatest grief,
Though little he do feel it, set down sharply.
Dispatch the most convenient messenger:
When haply he shall hear that she is gone, 35
He will return; and hope I may that she,
Hearing so much, will speed her foot again,
Led hither by pure love. Which of them both
Is dearest to me, I have no skill in sense
To make distinction. Provide this messenger. 40
My heart is heavy and mine age is weak;
Grief would have tears, and sorrow bids me speak.
[*Exeunt.*

SCENE V.—*Without the Walls of Florence.*

A tucket afar off. Enter old Widow of Florence, DIANA, VIOLENTA, *and* MARIANA, *with other Citizens.*

Wid. Nay, come; for if they do approach the city, we shall lose all the sight.

Dia. They say the French count has done most honourable service.

Wid. It is reported that he has taken their greatest 5
commander, and that with his own hand he slew
the duke's brother. [*Tucket.*] We have lost our

---

3. Dia.] Violenta. Cambridge Editors conj. Perhaps Violenta's part has been lost altogether, which may easily have happened. If not, it is difficult to find a place in the dialogue, in which she must necessarily have spoken. Perhaps it was she who said, "Come; let's return again, and suffice ourselves with the report of it," and she may then have gone away. It is to be supposed that she was not present at the end, for Helena does not invite her to dinner with the others, which she would probably have done had Violenta still been there. 7. [Tucket] Capell, omitted Ff.

labour; they are gone a contrary way: hark!
you may know by their trumpets.

Mar. Come; let's return again, and suffice ourselves 10
with the report of it. Well, Diana, take heed of
this French earl: the honour of a maid is her
name, and no legacy is so rich as honesty.

Wid. I have told my neighbour how you have been
solicited by a gentleman his companion. 15

Mar. I know that knave; hang him! one Parolles:
a filthy officer he is in those suggestions for the
young earl. Beware of them, Diana; their
promises, enticements, oaths, tokens, and all these
engines of lust, are not the things they go under: 20
many a maid hath been seduced by them; and
the misery is, example, that so terrible shows in
the wrack of maidenhood, cannot for all that
dissuade succession, but that they are limed with
the twigs that threatens them. I hope I need 25
not to advise you further; but I hope your own
grace will keep you where you are, though there
were no further danger known but the modesty
which is so lost.

Dia. You shall not need to fear me. 30

Enter HELENA.

Wid. I hope so. Look, here comes a pilgrim: I
know she will lie at my house; thither they send
one another. I'll question her.

22. *is, example,*] Rowe, *is example* Ff.

20. *go under*] profess to be. 24. *limed*] birdlime to catch birds.
24. *dissuade succession*] prevent 30. *fear me*] be anxious about me
imitation. An unusual use of the word. or be obliged to frighten me.

God save you, pilgrim! whither are you bound?
Hel. To S. Jaques le Grand. 35
   Where do the palmers lodge, I do beseech you?
Wid. At the S. Francis here beside the port.
Hel. Is this the way?
Wid.   Ay, marry, is't. Hark you!
                                     [A march afar off.
They come this way.
   If you will tarry, holy pilgrim, 40
But till the troops come by,
I will conduct you where you shall be lodg'd;
The rather, for I think I know your hostess
As ample as myself.
Hel.   Is it yourself?
Wid. If you shall please so, pilgrim. 45
Hel. I thank you, and will stay upon your leisure.
Wid. You came, I think, from France?
Hel.   I did so.
Wid. Here you shall see a countryman of yours
   That has done worthy service.
Hel.   His name, I pray you.

---

35. *le*] F 3, 4; *la* F 1, 2.

36. *palmers*] Reed explains: "Pilgrims that visited holy places; so called from a staff, or bough of palm they were wont to carry, especially such as had visited the holy places at Jerusalem. 'A pilgrim and a palmer differed thus: a pilgrim had some dwelling-place, the palmer none; the pilgrim travelled to some certain place, the palmer to all, and not to any one in particular; the pilgrim might go at his own charge, the palmer must profess wilful poverty; the pilgrim might give over his profession, the palmer must be constant, till he had the palm; that is, victory over his ghostly enemies, and life by death'" (Blount's *Glossography*, voce "Pilgrim").

37. *port*] gate. The word port is frequently used in this sense; cf. "Golden care that keepest the ports of slumber open wide" (*2 Henry IV.* IV. v. 24). See also *Antony and Cleopatra*, IV. iv. 23, and *Coriolanus*, I. vii. 1.

44. *ample*] I know your hostess as *well* as I know myself. Cf. "how ample you're beloved" (*Timon of Athens*, I. ii. 136).

Dia. The Count Rousillon: know you such a one? 50
Hel. But by the ear, that hears most nobly of him:
His face I know not.
Dia.   Whatsomere he is,
He's bravely taken here. He stole from France,
As 'tis reported, for the king had married him
Against his liking. Think you it is so? 55
Hel. Ay, surely, mere the truth: I know his lady.
Dia. There is a gentleman that serves the count
Reports but coarsely of her.
Hel.   What's his name?
Dia. Monsieur Parolles.
Hel.   O! I believe with him,
In argument of praise, or to the worth 60
Of the great count himself, she is too mean
To have her name repeated: all her deserving
Is a reserved honesty, and that
I have not heard examin'd.
Dia.   Alas! poor lady;
'Tis a hard bondage to become the wife 65
Of a detesting lord.
Wid. Ay, right; good creature, wheresoe'er she is,

---

52. *Whatsomere*] F 1; *What somere his is* F 2; *Whatsomere he is* F 3, 4.
56. *mere the*] *meerlye* Warburton, *the mere* Hanmer (S. Walker conj.).
58. *coarsely*] Johnson, *coursely* Ff.   67. *Ay, right: good creature*] Capell;
I write good creature F 1; *I right good creature* F 2, 3, 4.

52. *Whatsomere*] Cf. "all men's faces are true, whatsomere their hands are" (*Antony and Cleopatra*, II. vi. 102).
53. *bravely taken*] thought much of.
56. *mere the truth*] the plain truth. The Ff read "I, surely, meere the truth." I know of no other instance of "mere the," and it may be a misprint for "the mere." Warburton reads "meerlye" for "meere the."

60. *argument of praise*] as for deserving praise. . . .
63. *reserved honesty*] a well-guarded chastity. As in *Cymbeline*, I. iv. 143, "I will bring from thence that honour of hers which you imagine so reserved."
64. *examin'd*] questioned or doubted.
67. *Ay, . . . she is*] F 1 here reads "I write good creature"; the other Ff "I right good creature," which seems

Her heart weighs sadly. This young maid might do her
A shrewd turn if she pleas'd.

Hel. How do you mean? 70
May be the amorous count solicits her
In the unlawful purpose.

Wid. He does indeed;
And brokes with all that can in such a suit
Corrupt the tender honour of a maid:
But she is arm'd for him, and keeps her guard
In honestest defence.

Mar. The gods forbid else! 75

Enter, with drum and colours, the whole Florentine army, BERTRAM *and* PAROLLES.

Wid. So, now they come.
That is Antonio, the duke's eldest son;
That, Escalus.

Hel. Which is the Frenchman?

Dia. He;
That with the plume: 'tis a most gallant fellow;
I would he lov'd his wife. If he were honester 80

---

75. Enter . . . Parolles] before "Mar. *The gods forbid else!*" in Ff.

an improvement. Most editors have, however, adhered to the very obscure reading "I write," taking it to be a parallel to the "I write man" (II. iii. 200, above), or as meaning "I declare." Rolfe, who takes this last to be the best, accepts the reading only as a choice of evils, and suspects some corruption. Rowe has "Ah! right good creature!" and Theobald, "Ah! right; good creature!" Malone conjectures "I weet good creature," but seems to accept the reading "write," comparing it to "About it, and write happy when thou hast done," in *King Lear*.

69. *shrewd*] mischievous; not quite the same as in line 89, below, or in v. iii. 232, below. It is here used as in *Antony and Cleopatra*, IV. ix. 5, "the last day (of battle) was a shrewd one to us." Cf. also the old proverb, "God sendeth the shrewd cow short hornes" (J. Heywood, *Prov.* (Sharm.); p. 47).

He were much goodlier; is't not a handsome gentleman?
Hel. I like him well.
Dia. 'Tis pity he is not honest. Yond's that same knave
    That leads him to these places: were I his lady,
    I would poison that vile rascal.
Hel. Which is he? 85
Dia. That jack-an-apes with scarfs. Why is he melancholy?
Hel. Perchance he's hurt i' the battle.
Par. Lose our drum! well.
Mar. He's shrewdly vexed at something. Look, he
    has spied us. 90
Wid. Marry, hang you!
Mar. And your courtesy, for a ring-carrier!
    [*Exeunt Bertram, Parolles, Officers and Soldiers.*
Wid. The troop is past. Come, pilgrim, I will bring you
    Where you shall host: of enjoin'd penitents

81. *gentleman?*] F 2, 3, 4; Gentleman. F 1.   84. *places*] Ff, *passes* Dyce (Lettsom conj.).   93, 94. *bring you Where*] bring || you, Where F 1.

84. *places*] The emendation "passes" was first adopted by Dyce, and may be supported by "I perceive your grace, like power divine hath look'd upon my passes" (*Measure for Measure*, v. i. 375). The very doubtful reading of the Ff "places" is understood to mean common houses; which seems hardly probable, seeing that Diana's home had been visited.
86. *jack-an-apes*] "Precise origin uncertain . . . the word appears first as an opprobrious nickname of William de la Pole, Duke of Suffolk (murdered 1450), whose badge was a clog and chain, such as was attached to a tame ape . . . 'Jack Napes' is the earliest form, of which 'Jack-a-Napes,' 'Jack of Napes' (? Naples) 'Jack-an-Ape,' 'Jack and apes,' are later perversions. 1592, Greene, *Upstart Courtier*, H j b,

'A jollie light timberd Jacke a Napes in a sute of watchet Taffeta.' Cf. 1623, Massinger, *Bondman*, II. iii., 'Here's a Jane-of-apes shall serve'" (*New Eng. Dict.*).
89. *shrewdly vexed*] Schmidt compares this use of the word "shrewdly" to the German adverb *arg*. It occurs again below (v. iii. 232), "You boggle shrewdly," and in *Hamlet* (I. iv. 1), "The air bites shrewdly."
92. *ring-carrier*] a term of obloquy; cf. Bandello, *Tragical Discourses* (Tudor Classics, ed. Fenton, 1890), vol. i. p. 151, "the he bawd of London carryeth a ring in his mouth . . . the she bawd a basket" (W. J. C.).
94. *host*] find a host. Cf. "Go, bear it to the Centaur where we host" (*Comedy of Errors*, I. ii. 9).
94. *enjoin'd*] bound by an oath.

7

>   There's four or five, to Great S. Jaques bound, 95
>   Already at my house.
>
> *Hel.*   I humbly thank you.
>   Please it this matron and this gentle maid
>   To eat with us to-night, the charge and thanking
>   Shall be for me; and, to requite you further,
>   I will bestow some precepts of this virgin   100
>   Worthy the note.
>
> *Both.*   We'll take your offer kindly.
>   [*Exeunt.*

SCENE VI.—*Camp before Florence.*

Enter BERTRAM *and the two French Lords.*

First Lord. Nay, good my lord, put him to't: let him have his way.

Second Lord. If your lordship find him not a hilding, hold me no more in your respect.

First Lord. On my life, my lord, a bubble.   5

Ber. Do you think I am so far deceived in him?

First Lord. Believe it, my lord, in mine own direct knowledge, without any malice, but to speak of him as my kinsman, he's a most notable coward, an infinite and endless liar, an hourly promise-   10

---

100. *of*] F 1; *on* F 2, 3, 4.

Scene VI.

6. *Do . . . him?*] Pope's arrangement. In the Ff two lines, the first ending with *far*.

100. *of this virgin*] Cf. "What bestow of him" (*Twelfth Night*, III. iv. 2).

Scene VI.

3. *hilding*] a coward,—a term of extreme obloquy, applied also to beasts.

5. *bubble*] a deceptive thing, as in Swift's phrase, "The nation then too late will find . . . South Sea at best a mighty bubble." Cf. also "bubble reputation."

9. *as my kinsman*] as of my kinsman.

breaker, the owner of no one good quality worthy
your lordship's entertainment.

Second Lord. It were fit you knew him; lest, reposing
too far in his virtue, which he hath not, he might
at some great and trusty business in a main   15
danger fail you.

Ber. I would I knew in what particular action to try
him.

Second Lord. None better than to let him fetch off
his drum, which you hear him so confidently   20
undertake to do.

First Lord. I, with a troop of Florentines, will suddenly surprise him: such I will have whom I am
sure he knows not from the enemy. We will
bind and hoodwink him so, that he shall suppose   25
no other but that he is carried into the leaguer
of the adversaries, when we bring him to our own
tents. Be but your lordship present at his ex-
amination: if he do not, for the promise of his
life and in the highest compulsion of base fear,   30
offer to betray you and deliver all the intelligence
in his power against you, and that with the
divine forfeit of his soul upon oath, never trust
my judgment in any thing.

13. *lest,*] F 4; *least,* F 1, 2, 3.   26. *leaguer*] F 4; *Leager* F 1, 2, 3.

12. *entertainment*] Cf. below, IV. i. 15, "band of strangers i' the adversary's entertainment." Bacon's *Henry VII.,* "He was . . . an entertainer of fortune by the day."

19, 20. *fetch off his drum*] It must be remembered that the loss of drums in those days was a matter of great importance, because they were decorated with the colours of the regiment. The loss was therefore equivalent to the loss of the colours.

26. *leaguer*] Douce quotes Sir John Smythe's *Discourses*: "They will not vouchsafe in their speeches or writings to use our ancient terms belonging to matters of warre, but doo call a campe by the Dutch name of 'Legar'; nor will not affoord to say, that such a towne or such a fort is besieged, but that it is 'belegard.'"

Second Lord. O! for the love of laughter, let him 35
fetch his drum: he says he has a stratagem for 't.
When your lordship sees the bottom of his success in 't, and to what metal this counterfeit lump
of ore will be melted, if you give him not John
*Drum's entertainment, your inclining cannot be 40
removed. Here he comes.

Enter PAROLLES.

First Lord. [*Aside to Bert.*] O! for the love of
laughter, hinder not the honour of his design:
let him fetch off his drum in any hand.

37. *his*] Rowe, *this* Ff.   39. *ore*] *oar* Theobald, *ours* Ff, *ores* Collier MS.
42. [Aside . . .] Capell, omitted Ff.   43. *honour*] *humour* Theobald.

39, 40. *John Drum's entertainment*] the same as Tom Drum's. Various passages have been collected in which this expression occurs. Theobald quotes from "an old motley interlude" (printed in 1601) called *Jack Drum's Entertainment; or, The Comedy of Pasquil and Catherine.* In this Jack Drum is a servant of intrigue who is ever aiming at projects, and always foiled and given the drop. Also an- other old piece (published in 1627) called *Apollo Shroving*, in which occurs: "Tom Drum's entertainment: a flap with a fox-tail. . . ." Holinshed in his description of Ireland, speaking of Patrick Sarsefield (Mayor of Dublin in 1551) and of his extravagant hospi- tality, subjoins that "no guest had ever a cold or forbidding look: so that his porter durst not for both his eares give the simplest man that resorted to his house, Tom Drum his entertayn- ment, which is, to hale a man in by the heade, and thrust him out by both the shoulders." Malone quotes a passage from the above-mentioned motley in- terlude : "In faith good gentlemen, I think we shall be forced to give you right John Drum's entertainment (*i.e.* treat you very ill) . . ." Reed finds in Taylor's *Laugh and be Fat*, "Monsʳ Odcome Who on his owne backe-side receiv'd his pay Not like the enter- tainmᵗ of Jacke Drum Who was best welcome when he went away." Also in *Manners and Customs of all Nations* (ed. Aston, 1611, 4to, p. 280), "Some others on the contrarie part, give them John Drum's intertainmᵗ reviling and beating them away from their houses." But little clew is given as to the origin of the phrase except in such phrases as "Oh, it's a most precious fool, make much of him. I can com- pare him to nothing more happly than a drum, for everyone may play upon him" (Jonson, *Every Man in his Humour*, III. i.).

44. *in any hand*] Cf. with this phrase "at any hand" (*Taming of the Shrew*, I. ii. 147, 227), and "Of all hands" (*Love's Labour's Lost*, IV. iii. 219). The expression "in any hand" occurs over and over again in Holland's *Pliny* (pp. 456, 508, 553, etc.).

sc. vi.] THAT ENDS WELL 101

Ber. How now, monsieur! this drum sticks sorely in 45
    your disposition.
Second Lord. A pox on't! let it go: 'tis but a drum.
Par. "But a drum!" Is't "but a drum"? A drum
    so lost! There was excellent command,—to
    charge in with our horse upon our own wings, 50
    and to rend our own soldiers!
Second Lord. That was not to be blamed in the
    command of the service: it was a disaster of war
    that Cæsar himself could not have prevented, if
    he had been there to command. 55
Ber. Well, we cannot greatly condemn our success:
    some dishonour we had in the loss of that drum;
    but it is not to be recovered.
Par. It might have been recovered.
Ber. It might; but it is not now. 60
Par. It is to be recovered. But that the merit of
    service is seldom attributed to the true and exact
    performer, I would have that drum or another, or
    hic jacet.
Ber. Why, if you have a stomach, to't, monsieur; if 65
    you think your mystery in stratagem can bring
    this instrument of honour again into his native
    quarter, be magnanimous in the enterprise and
    go on; I will grace the attempt for a worthy

---

65. *a stomach, to't, monsieur; if*] *a stomacke, too't Monsieur: if* F 1; *a stomacke: too't Monsieur: if* F 2; *a stomach to't, Monsieur: if* F 3, 4. 68. *magnanimous*] *magnanimious* F 1.

49. *There was an excellent command*] we were exceedingly well commanded —used sarcastically of course.
66. *mystery in stratagem*] Schmidt places this instance of the word mystery under a separate heading, meaning professional skill. The word may be compared with "craft," which is still used in much the same way.

exploit: if you speed well in it, the duke shall 70
both speak of it, and extend to you what further
becomes his greatness, even to the utmost syllable
of your worthiness.

Par. By the hand of a soldier, I will undertake it.

Ber. But you must not now slumber in it. 75

Par. I'll about it this evening: and I will presently
pen down my dilemmas, encourage myself in my
certainty, put myself into my mortal preparation,
and by midnight look to hear further from me.

Ber. May I be bold to acquaint his grace you are 80
gone about it?

Par. I know not what the success will be, my lord;
but the attempt I vow.

Ber. I know th' art valiant; and to the possibility
of thy soldiership, will subscribe for thee. Fare- 85
well.

Par. I love not many words. [*Exit.*

First Lord. No more than a fish loves water. Is not
this a strange fellow, my lord, that so confidently
seems to undertake this business, which he knows 90

---

81. *it?*] Rowe (ed. 2), *it.* Ff.

77. *dilemmas*] occurs only twice in Shakespeare. Cf. "In perplexity and doubtful dilemma" (*Merry Wives,* IV. v. 87). The word seems to be used in its primitive sense of "an argument equally conclusive by contrary suppositions." He was going to pen them down in order to argue them out in his favour, "encourage himself in his certainty."

78. *mortal preparation*] preparation for the end of mortal life. Cf. "pay his breath to time and mortal custom" (*Macbeth,* IV. i. 100). A schoolboy might idiomatically substitute "mortal funk."

84. *the possibility*] the capability. Johnson quotes from Rogers, "Example not only teaches us our duty, but convinces us of the possibility of our imitation."

87. *I love . . . words*] This passage supports the conjecture that Parolles' name is derived from the French *paroles.* It is, however, a trisyllable, it having been thus pronounced at that time in England. Cotgrave writes *parolles.*

is not to be done; damns himself to do, and
dares better be damned than to do 't?
Second Lord. You do not know him, my lord, as we
do: certain it is that he will steal himself into a
man's favour, and for a week escape a great deal   95
of discoveries; but when you find him out, you
have him ever after.
Ber. Why, do you think he will make no deed at all of
this that so seriously he does address himself unto?
First Lord. None in the world; but return with an   100
invention, and clap upon you two or three probable lies. But we have almost embossed him,
you shall see his fall to-night; for indeed he is
not for your lordship's respect.
Second Lord. We'll make you some sport with the   105
fox ere we case him. He was first smoked by
the old lord Lafeu: when his disguise and he is
parted, tell me what a sprat you shall find him;
which you shall see this very night.
First Lord. I must go look my twigs: he shall be   110
caught.

92. *do 't ?*] Theobald; *doo 't* F 1, 2; *do 't* F. 3, 4.   96. *discoveries*] *discovery* S. Walker (conj.); *out*] *once* Daniel (conj.).   101, 102. *probable*] *improbable* S. Walker (conj.), *palpable* Proescholdt.   110, 111. *I . . . caught*] given to the former speaker by Capell. One line in Pope; two in Ff, the first ending with *twigs*.

95. *deal*] Not often used with a plural. *New Eng. Dict.* gives, 1597, Gerarde, *Herbal*, I. xxxi. § 1, 42, "Nothing else but a deale of flocks set and thrust togither."
102. *embossed*] "To emboss a deer is to enclose him in a wood" (Johnson).
106. *case him*] strip him naked. Cf. "Pompey is uncasing for the combat" (*Love's Labour's Lost*, v. ii. 707). *New Eng. Dict.* gives, 1803, Rees. Cycl.

s.v. Casing, "They say, flay a deer, case a hare."
106. *smoked*] Cf. IV. i. 28, below, "They begin to smoke me." Johnson gives two instances from Addison: "Will Trippet begins to be smoked"— "I began to smoke that they were a parcel of mummers." Also from Hudibras, "He hither came to observe and smoke." The meaning is obvious.
110. *I . . . twigs*] The metaphor of

104 ALL'S WELL [ACT III.

Ber. Your brother he shall go along with me.
First Lord. As 't please your lordship: I 'll leave you.
                [*Exit.*
Ber. Now will I lead you to the house, and show you
 The lass I spoke of.
Second Lord.   But you say she's honest. 115
Ber. That's all the fault. I spoke with her but once,
 And found her wondrous cold; but I sent to her,
 By this same coxcomb that we have i' the wind,
 Tokens and letters which she did resend;
 And this is all I have done. She's a fair creature; 120
 Will you go see her?
Second Lord.   With all my heart, my lord.
                [*Exeunt.*

SCENE VII.—*Florence. A Room in the Widow's
        House.*

Enter HELENA *and* Widow.

Hel. If you misdoubt me that I am not she,
 I know not how I shall assure you further,
 But I shall lose the grounds I work upon.
Wid. Though my estate be fall'n, I was well born,
 Nothing acquainted with these businesses; 5

113. Exit] Theobald, omitted Ff.

Scene VII.

5. *businesses*] *basenesses* Anon. conj.

limed twigs, as above, III. v. 24. "Look" is used transitively, as often elsewhere.
118. *have i' the wind*] a proverbial saying akin to the modern phrase "to be in the wind of."

Scene VII.

3. *lose the grounds*] Helena could give no further proof of her identity, save by revealing herself to the Count himself—the very thing she did not wish to do.

	And would not put my reputation now
	In any staining act.
Hel.	Nor would I wish you.
	First, give me trust, the count he is my husband,
	And what to your sworn counsel I have spoken
	Is so from word to word; and then you cannot, 10
	By the good aid that I of you shall borrow,
	Err in bestowing it.
Wid.	I should believe you;
	For you have show'd me that which well approves
	You're great in fortune.
Hel.	Take this purse of gold,
	And let me buy your friendly help thus far, 15
	Which I will over-pay and pay again
	When I have found it. The count he woos your daughter,
	Lays down his wanton siege before her beauty,
	Resolved to carry her: let her in fine consent,
	As we'll direct her how 'tis best to bear it. 20
	Now his important blood will nought deny
	That she'll demand: a ring the county wears,
	That downward hath succeeded in his house
	From son to son, some four or five descents

8. *count he*] *County* Dyce (S. Walker conj.), also line 17, below.   14. *You're*] *Y' are* Ff.   19. *Resolved*] Collier; *Resolue* F 1; *Resolves* F 2, 3, 4.

9. *your sworn counsel*] Schmidt explains "counsel" as being "privity to another's secret thoughts," as when Othello says, "He was of my counsel in my whole course of wooing" (III. iii. 111). "Sworn counsel" = bound by oath to secrecy.

21. *important blood*] Johnson calls this a corrupt use of the word, but it seems to tally singularly well with the French *emportant*. Shakespeare uses it frequently in this sense: "your important letters" (*Comedy of Errors*, v. i. 138); "if the prince be too important, tell him there is measure in every thing" (*Much Ado*, II. i. 74). See W. J. Craig's note on *King Lear*, IV. iv. 26.

22. *county*] count, as elsewhere.

Since the first father wore it: this ring he holds . 25
In most rich choice; yet in his idle fire,
To buy his will, it would not seem too dear,
Howe'er repented after.
Wid.   Now I see
 The bottom of your purpose.
Hel. You see it lawful then. It is no more,   30
But that your daughter, ere she seems as won,
Desires this ring; appoints him an encounter;
In fine, delivers me to fill the time,
Herself most chastely absent. After this,
To marry her, I'll add three thousand crowns   35
To what is past already.
Wid.   I have yielded.
Instruct my daughter how she shall persever,
That time and place with this deceit so lawful
May prove coherent. Every night he comes
With musics of all sorts and songs compos'd   40
To her unworthiness: it nothing steads us
To chide him from our eaves, for he persists
As if his life lay on 't.
Hel.   Why then to-night
Let us assay our plot; which, if it speed,
Is wicked meaning in a lawful deed,   45
And lawful meaning in a lawful act,

28, 29. *Now . . . purpose*] Capell's arrangement; in one line in the Ff.
34. *After this*] F 2, 3, 4; *after* F 1.   41. *steads*] F 4; *steeds* F 1, 2, 3.
46. *lawful meaning*] *unlawful meaning* Hanmer; *a lawful act*] *a wicked act* Warburton, *a lawless act* Anon. conj.

26. *In most rich choice*] in very high esteem. Cf. Evelyn's *Kalendar,* "Carry into the shade such auriculas, seedlings or plants, as are for their choiceness reserved in pots."

26. *idle*] See II. v. 51, above.
40, 41. *compos'd To her unworthiness*] composed with unworthy purpose to her.

Where both not sin, and yet a sinful fact.
But let's about it. [*Exeunt.*

ACT IV

SCENE I.—*Without the Florentine Camp.*

Enter Second French Lord, with five or six Soldiers in ambush.

Second Lord. He can come no other way but by this hedge-corner. When you sally upon him, speak what terrible language you will: though you understand it not yourselves; no matter; for we must not seem to understand him, unless some one among   5
us, whom we must produce for an interpreter.
First Sold. Good captain, let me be the interpreter.
Second Lord. Art not acquainted with him? knows he not thy voice?
First Sold. No, sir, I warrant you.   10

Enter Second French Lord] Camb. Edd. ; Enter one of the Frenchmen Ff. See note on Act II. Scene i.   1. Sec. Lord] 1 Lord E. Ff.   7. *captain*] F 3, 4; *captaine* F 1; *captiue* F 2.

47. *Where . . . fact*] Either corrupt or purposely obscure. The meaning of the whole passage as it stands seems to be that the deed is lawful and yet is meant to be wrong by Bertram; that both happen to be innocent—and yet guilty, he of wantonness, she of deception. If any change be called for we might read "and yet a sin full act."

Act IV. Scene I.

2. *hedge-corner*] In Shakespeare's day hedges were not frequent: the country was not generally enclosed until long after, and so a hedge surrounding a garden or field would be a prominent object, and one to which a hunted animal would escape for refuge.

Second Lord. But what linsey-woolsey hast thou to
    speak to us again?
First Sold. E'en such as you speak to me.
Second Lord. He must think us some band of strangers
    i' the adversary's entertainment. Now he hath 15
    a smack of all neighbouring languages; therefore
    we must every one be a man of his own fancy,
    not to know what we speak one to another; so
    we seem to know, is to know straight our pur-
    pose: choughs' language, gabble enough, and 20
    good enough. As for you, interpreter, you must
    seem very politic. But couch, ho! here he comes,
    to beguile two hours in a sleep, and then to return
    and swear the lies he forges.

            Enter PAROLLES.

Par. Ten o'clock: within these three hours 'twill be 25
    time enough to go home. What shall I say I
    have done? It must be a very plausive inven-
    tion that carries it. They begin to smoke me,

---

15. *adversary's*] Johnson, *adversaries* Ff, *adversaries'* Warburton. 20. *choughs'*] F 3, 4; *choughs* F 1, 2.

11. *linsey-woolsey*] An unintelligible mixture of several languages. Johnson quotes Hudibras, "A lawless linsey-woolsey brother Half of one order, half another." The *New Eng. Dict.* traces this word back to the Cath. Aug. 1483 (*Old Eng. Lat. Dict.*), and the *Dial. Dict.* says it is alive in Hereford near the Welsh border. Also in Cumberland in the form of "Listy-wunsty."
14, 15. *strangers . . . entertainment*] foreign troops in the enemy's pay (Johnson). Cf. note on III. vi. 12, above.
19. *know straight*] Hanmer reads "shew straight," and Collier "Go straight to." The expression "know straight" seems here to mean "know our mind, our purpose." Malone would explain it, "Our seeming to know what we speak one to another is to make him to know our purpose immediately; to discover our design to him."
20. *choughs' language*] jackdaws' gabble.
27. *plausive*] plausible. Shakespeare uses both words indiscriminately.
28. *smoke me*] See note above, III. vi. 106.

and disgraces have of late knocked too often at
my door. I find my tongue is too foolhardy; 30
but my heart hath the fear of Mars before it and
of his creatures, not daring the reports of my
tongue.

Second Lord. This is the first truth that e'er thine own
tongue was guilty of. 35

Par. What the devil should move me to undertake
the recovery of this drum, being not ignorant of
the impossibility, and knowing I had no such
purpose? I must give myself some hurts, and
say I got them in exploit. Yet slight ones will 40
not carry it: they will say, "Came you off with
so little?" and great ones I dare not give. Wherefore, what's the instance? Tongue, I must put
you into a butter-woman's mouth, and buy myself
another of Bajazet's mule, if you prattle me into 45
these perils.

Second Lord. Is it possible he should know what he
is, and be that he is?

Par. I would the cutting of my garments would serve
the turn, or the breaking of my Spanish sword. 50

Second Lord. We cannot afford you so.

---

40. *in exploit*] *in the exploit* W. J. Craig (conj.). 45. *Bajazet's*] *Baiazeth's* F 1; *Baiazeths* F 2, 3, 4; *Balaam's* Addis conj.; *mule*] F 1, 2; *mules* F 3, 4; *mute* Hanmer (Warburton). 48. *is?*] F 4; *is.* F 1, 2, 3.

43. *what's the instance?*] Parolles asks himself, what proof can he possibly give? "What instance gives Lord Warwick for his vow?" (*2 Henry VI.* III. ii. 159); "I have received a certain instance that Glendower is dead" (*2 Henry IV.* III. i. 103), etc.

45. *Bajazet's mule*] Parolles is meditating on the possibility of having to get rid of his tongue because it wags too much, and to buy a less talkative one. But why he should buy from Bajazet's mule is a mystery. Hanmer read "mute," and explained, "I'll buy a tongue that never speaks."

51. *afford you so*] we cannot afford it to you so, we cannot allow you to have it so cheap.

Par. Or the baring of my beard, and to say it was in
  stratagem.
Second Lord. 'Twould not do.
Par. Or to drown my clothes, and say I was stripped.   55
Second Lord. Hardly serve.
Par. Though I swore I leaped from the window of
  the citadel—
Second Lord. How deep?
Par. Thirty fathom.   60
Second Lord. Three great oaths would scarce make
  that be believed.
Par. I would I had any drum of the enemy's: I
  would swear I recovered it.
Second Lord. You shall hear one anon.   65
Par. A drum now of the enemy's,—   [*Alarum within.*
Second Lord. *Throca movousus, cargo, cargo, cargo.*
All. *Cargo, cargo, cargo, villianda par corbo, cargo.*
Par. O! ransom, ransom! Do not hide mine eyes.
      [*They seize and blindfold him.*
First Sold. *Boskos thromuldo boskos.*   70
Par. I know you are the Muskos' regiment;
  And I shall lose my life for want of language.
  If there be here German, or Dane, low Dutch,

---

52. *baring*] *paring* F 4.   58. *citadel*—] Theobald, *citadell.* Ff.   60. *fathom*] Rowe, *fadome* Ff.   66. *enemy's,*—] Camb. Edd., *enemy's!* Malone, *enemies!* Theobald, *enemies.* Ff.   69. *O . . . eyes*] Pope's arrangement; two lines in Ff; They . . . him] Rowe, omitted Ff.   70. *First Soldier*] throughout these scenes described as "Interpreter" in the Ff.   71. *Muskos*] Capell, *Muskos* Ff.

---

52. *baring*] shaving. "Shave the head and tie the beard, and say it was the desire of the penitent to be so bared before his death" (*Measure for Measure*, IV. ii. 189).

53. *stratagem*] the carrying out of the stratagem. Cf. III. vi. 66, above.

55. *drown*] Cf. *Tempest*, v. i. 57, "I'll drown my book."

Italian, or French, let him speak to me:
I will discover that which shall undo 75
The Florentine.
First Sold. *Boskos vauvado*: I understand thee, and
can speak thy tongue: *Kerelybonto,* Sir, betake
thee to thy faith, for seventeen poniards are at
thy bosom. 80
Par. O!
First Sold. O! pray, pray, pray. *Manka revania dulche.*
Second Lord. *Oscorbidulchos volivorco.*
First Sold. The general is content to spare thee yet;
And, hoodwink'd as thou art, will lead thee on 85
To gather from thee: haply thou may'st inform
Something to save thy life.
Par. O! let me live,
And all the secrets of our camp I'll show,
Their force, their purposes; nay, I'll speak that
Which you will wonder at.
First Sold. But wilt thou faithfully? 90
Par. If I do not, damn me.
First Sold. *Acordo linta.*
Come on; thou art granted space.
 [*Exit, with Parolles guarded.*
 A short alarum within.
Second Lord. Go, tell the Count Rousillon, and my brother,
We have caught the woodcock, and will keep him
muffled
Till we do hear from them.

75, 76.] Arranged as in Malone; one line in Ff.

82. *pray, pray*] Used in the same connection as "betake thee to thy faith."

94. *woodcock*] a bird supposed to have no brains, and often used instead of "fool."

Second Sold.   Captain, I will.   95
Second Lord. A' will betray us all unto ourselves:
    Inform on that.
Second Sold. So I will, sir.
Second Lord. Till then I'll keep him dark and safely
    lock'd.   [*Exeunt.*

SCENE II.—*Florence. A Room in the Widow's
House.*

Enter BERTRAM *and* DIANA.

Ber. They told me that your name was Fontibell.
Dia. No, my good lord, Diana.
Ber.   Titled goddess;
    And worth it, with addition! But, fair soul,
    In your fine frame hath love no quality?
    If the quick fire of youth light not your mind,   5
    You are no maiden, but a monument:
    When you are dead you should be such a one
    As you are now, for you are cold and stern;
    And now you should be as your mother was
    When your sweet self was got.   10
Dia. She then was honest.
Ber.   So should you be.

97. *Inform on that*] *inform 'em that* Rowe and Dyce.
Scene II.
Enter . . .] Enter Bertram and the Maide called Diana Ff.   2. *Titled goddess;*] *Titl'd, goddess* Capell.   6. *monument.*] *monument.* F 1.

97. *Inform on that*] Dyce says, "It appears to me that the context positively requires ''em.'"
Scene II.
11. *should*] means "would,"

Dia.   No:
My mother did but duty; such, my lord,
As you owe to your wife.
Ber.   No more o' that!
I prithee do not strive against my vows.
I was compell'd to her; but I love thee   15
By love's own sweet constraint, and will for ever
Do thee all rights of service.
Dia.   Ay, so you serve us
Till we serve you; but when you have our roses,
You barely leave our thorns to prick ourselves,
And mock us with our bareness.
Ber.   How have I sworn! 20
Dia. 'Tis not the many oaths that makes the truth,
But the plain single vow that is vow'd true.
What is not holy, that we swear not by,
But take the high'st to witness: then, pray you, tell me,
If I should swear by Jove's great attributes,   25
I lov'd your dearly, would you believe my oaths,

19. *barely*] *basely* Rowe (ed. 2), *merely* Lettsom conj.   25. *Jove's*] F 3, 4; *Iouss* F 1, 2; *God's* Globe ed. (Camb. Edd. conj.); *love's* Grant White (Johnson conj.).

14. *my vows*] Malone quotes Webster, *Vittoria Corombona* (1612), "Henceforth I'll never lie with thee, My vow is fix'd"; implying that the present passage is to be understood in the same sense.

21. etc.] This passage has been held to be corrupt by many editors. In line 25 Johnson said he could hardly distinguish whether the word in F 1 was *Jove* or *Love*. *Jove*, the more difficult version of the two, has been accepted, and I think there can be no doubt that that is the word printed in the 1623 Folio. But it is possible that Shakespeare wrote *love*: possible also that he wrote *God*, and that, as Haliwell conjectured, *God* was erased on account of the law against profanity. The whole passage lends itself to emendation. Staunton proposed to give Bertram the words, "Then . . . ill?" and Johnson, "What . . . witness." In the Collier MS. the whole passage from "What is . . . against him" is erased.

8

When I did love you ill? This has no holding,
To swear by him whom I protest to love,
That I will work against him: therefore your oaths
Are words and poor conditions, but unseal'd;   30
At least in my opinion.

Ber.   Change it, change it.
Be not so holy-cruel: love is holy;
And my integrity ne'er knew the crafts
That you do charge men with. Stand no more off,
But give thyself unto my sick desires,   35
Who then recovers: say thou art mine, and ever
My love as it begins shall so persever.

Dia. [I see that men make rope's in such a scarre
That we'll forsake ourselves.] Give me that ring.

Ber. I'll lend it thee, my dear; but have no power   40
To give it from me.

Dia.   Will you not, my lord?

---

28. *To swear . . . love*] To swear (*by Him*) *that I will work against him Whom I protest to love* (Addis conj.); *by him*] *to him* Rann (Johnson conj.); *whom*] *when* Singer; *protest*] *attest* Johnson conj., *profess* Harris conj., Becket proposes "and to protest I love Whom I will work against." 29. *That I will . . .*] *While that I did* Herr conj., Hudson conj. omitted "him." 30. *but*] *best* Williams conj., *yet* Herr conj. 32. *holy-cruel*] Theobald, *holy cruell* Ff. 38, 39. [*I see . . . ourselves*] *make rope's in such a scarre* F 1, 2; *make ropes in such a scarre* F 3; *make ropes in such a scar* F 4. More than a score of readings are to be found in various editions (Cambridge ed. gives twenty-five).

27. *holding*] consistency (Johnson and Schmidt). Cf. "Thou sayest well, and it holds well too" (*1 Henry IV.* I. ii. 34).

28. *by him*] to him.

32. *holy-cruel*] This is a strange expression, and possibly corrupt. Perhaps we should read "wholly cruel." The play on the words gives some support to the conjecture.

36. *Who then recovers*] "Who" refers either to Bertram's self (in which case this is another instance of phrase logically but not grammatically correct), or else to the desires, which involves two unusual constructions—"who" after "desires" and a singular verb.

38.] No emendation has yet been proposed which is quite satisfactory and clears away all the difficulties of a passage which is, without doubt, corrupt. It is generally supposed that the phrase must convey some excuse for asking for the ring, for the sudden change of tactics.

Ber. It is an honour longing to our house,
   Bequeathed down from many ancestors,
   Which were the greatest obloquy i' the world
   In me to lose.
Dia.   Mine honour's such a ring: 45
   My chastity's the jewel of our house,
   Bequeathed down from many ancestors,
   Which were the greatest obloquy i' the world
   In me to lose. Thus your own proper wisdom
   Brings in the champion honour on my part 50
   Against your vain assault.
Ber   Here, take my ring:
   My house, mine honour, yea, my life, be thine,
   And I'll be bid by thee.
Dia. When midnight comes, knock at my chamber-window:
   I'll order take my mother shall not hear. 55
   Now will I charge you in the band of truth,
   When you have conquer'd my yet maiden bed,
   Remain there but an hour, nor speak to me.
   My reasons are most strong; and you shall know them
   When back again this ring shall be deliver'd: 60
   And on your finger in the night I'll put
   Another ring, that what in time proceeds
   May token to the future our past deeds.
   Adieu, till then; then, fail not. You have won
   A wife of me, though there my hope be done. 65
Ber. A heaven on earth I have won by wooing thee.
                                              [*Exit.*
Dia. For which live long to thank both heaven and me!

42. *longing*] belonging, as often in Shakespeare.   56. *band of truth*] Cf. "Thy oath and band" (= bond) (*Richard II.* I. i. 2).

116   ALL'S WELL   [ACT IV.

You may so in the end.
My mother told me just how he would woo,
As if she sat in 's heart; she says all men   70
Have the like oaths: he had sworn to marry me
When his wife's dead; therefore I'll lie with him
When I am buried. Since Frenchmen are so braid,
Marry that will, I live and die a maid:
Only in this disguise I think 't no sin   75
To cozen him that would unjustly win.   [*Exit.*

SCENE III.—*The Florentine Camp.*

Enter the two French Lords, and some two or three Soldiers.

First Lord. You have not given him his mother's
    letter?
Second Lord. I have delivered it an hour since: there

---

71. *had*] Ff, *has* Dyce, *hath* Capell.   74. *I*] F 1, 2; *I'le* F 3, 4.

Scene III.

2. *letter?*] Rowe, *letter* Ff.

71. *he had*] he would have.
73. *braid*] Of doubtful meaning. Steevens quotes Greene, *Never too Late* (1616), "Dian rose with all her maids Blushing thus at love his braids." Also Thomas Drant's translation of Horace's *Epistles*, "Professing thee a friend, to plaie the ribbalde at a brade." In the *Romaunt of the Rose*, v. 1336, "braid seems to mean forthwith or at a jerk, answering the French *tantôt*. Cf. "The Ancient Song of Lytyl Thanke" (MS. Cotton, *Titus Andronicus*, xxvi.), "But in come ffrankelyn at a braid"=on a sudden. Boswell thinks Mr. Boaden's suggestion may be correct, namely, that it means fickle, apt to start away suddenly from engagements. "To braid" for to start is found in Lord Buckhurst and many old writers. Richardson makes it mean violent. Webster derives it from "to braid," knit, hence knit a net, draw into a net, deceive. Schmidt and Johnson also give deceitful. In *Pericles*, I. i. 93, we find, "'twould braid yourself too near for me to tell it," in which case, if we allow the analogy, the phrase means "since Frenchmen are so blamed, accused." The *New Eng. Dict.* throws no new light on this word "of doubtful meaning and origin," which proves how difficult it is to obtain new illustrations of its use.

is something in 't that stings his nature; for on the
reading it he changed almost into another man.   5

First Lord. He has much worthy blame laid upon him
for shaking off so good a wife and so sweet a lady.

Second Lord. Especially he hath incurred the everlasting displeasure of the king, who had even tuned
his bounty to sing happiness to him. I will tell you   10
a thing, but you shall let it dwell darkly within you.

First Lord. When you have spoken it, 'tis dead, and
I am the grave of it.

Second Lord. He hath perverted a young gentlewoman
here in Florence, of a most chaste renown; and this   15
night he fleshes his will in the spoil of her honour:
he hath given her his monumental ring, and thinks
himself made in the unchaste composition.

First Lord. Now, God delay our rebellion! as we are
ourselves, what things are we.   20

19. *delay*] *allay* Hanmer; *rebellion! as*] *rebellion,* as F 3, 4; *rebellion* as F 1, 2.

5. *another man*] Karl Elze understands this to mean moral change.
More probably it means merely growing pale. Mr. W. J. Craig quotes,
"At the reading of the letter he looked
like a man of another world" (*Jew of
Malta,* IV. iv. 67).

6. *worthy*] deserved. "This superficial tale is but a preface of her worthy
praise" (*1 Henry VI.* v. v. 11). Also,
"Hate turns one or both to worthy
danger and deserved death" (*Richard
II.* v. i. 68).

16. *fleshes*] satiates. Cf. "The wild
dog shall flesh his tooth on every
innocent" (*2 Henry IV.* IV. v. 133).
Also, Jonson's *Every Man in his
Humour* (II. ii.), "*Brainworm.* I am
fleshed now I have sped so well."

17. *monumental*] preserving memory.
Cf. the use of "monument" in Pope's
letter to Swift, "Collect the best
monuments of our friends, their own
images in their own writings."

18. *made . . .*] a made man=a
fortunate man. Cf. *Othello,* I. ii. 51,
"he's made for ever." (Also *Midsummer Night's Dream,* IV. ii. 18.)

18. *composition*] pact. Cf. "The
twelfth of August, Shoonehouen was
by composition yielded to the enemie
(1575). In August the Prince of Conde
with his armie . . . tooke Ruermonde
and Lennen by composition" (*A Briefe
Cronicle . . . of the Low Countries,
Germanie, Italy, etc.* 1598). Cf. I. i.
209, above.

19. *delay*] Hanmer would read
"allay": surely the original is correct.
"May God make us slow to rebel."
Dr. Hudson quotes Spenser, *The Faerie
Queene,* ii. 6, 40, "The hasty heat of
his avowd revenge delayd." And in
his 30th Sonnet, "That my exceeding

Second Lord. Merely our own traitors: and as in the common course of all treasons, we still see them reveal themselves, till they attain to their abhorred ends, so he that in this action contrives against his own nobility, in his proper stream o'erflows himself. 25

First Lord. Is it not meant damnable in us, to be trumpeters of our unlawful intents? We shall not then have his company to-night?

Second Lord. Not till after midnight, for he is dieted to his hour. 30

First Lord. That approaches apace: I would gladly have him see his company anatomized, that he

21. *in*] *is* Keightley conj. 23. *till*] *ere* Hanmer, *when* Mason conj., *while* W. J. Craig conj. 25.] Punctuation by Theobald; *nobility in . . . stream*, Ff.
27. *meant damnable*] Ff; Hanmer reads "most damnable," an emendation accepted by S. Walker, Dyce, and Proescholdt. 31. *dieted*] *tied* Daniel conj.
33. *company*] *companion* Hanmer.

heat is not delayd by her hart-frosen cold." In support of "allay" Williams says: "It is not . . . clear why the First Lord should wish such rebellions to be delayed, as no advantage could arise from mere postponement, and the poet himself warns us that 'delays have dangerous ends.' The error probably originated in a very pardonable mishearing of the first two letters. I read—Now God allay our rebellion. Cf. *Henry VIII.* I. i. 149, 'If with the sap of reason you would quench, Or but allay, the fire of passion . . .' If it be urged that delay (French, *délayer*) was originally the same as allay, I can only reply that, although Spenser may thus have used it, Shakespeare appears nowhere to have so employed it."

19, 20. *are ourselves*] unaided by God.

23, 24. *abhorred ends*] The meaning of the passage seems to be: "Just as in common course of all treasons, we always see them betray themselves and, in the long-run, come to their awful punishments, so Bertram, who by this deed alone contrives against his own nobility, covers himself still more in shame by publishing it." This is borne out by the next passage, "Is it not meant damnable in us to be the trumpeters" (etc.). Steevens takes "abhorred ends" to mean "the loathsome ends they aim at." Delius says that "till"=before. The construction is not an easy one to translate exactly.

27. *Is it . . . in us*] "Do we not willingly incur damnation by being trumpeters of . . . ?" Schmidt explains it, "Is not our drift a damnable one?" With the expression "meant damnable" cf. our phrase "I meant good" (evil).

31. *dieted*] perhaps corrupt; if not, it must mean "fully occupied." Daniel conjectures "tied to his hour," and quotes, "I'll not be tied to hours nor 'pointed times" (*Taming of the Shrew*, III. i. 19).

33. *company*] Parolles.

might take a measure of his own judgments,
wherein so curiously he had set this counterfeit.   35
Second Lord. We will not meddle with him till he come,
for his presence must be the whip of the other.
First Lord. In the meantime, what hear you of these
wars?
Second Lord. I hear there is an overture of peace.   40
First Lord. Nay, I assure you, a peace concluded.
Second Lord. What will Count Rousillon do then?
will he travel higher, or return again into France?
First Lord. I perceive by this demand, you are not
altogether of his council.   45
Second Lord. Let it be forbid, sir; so should I be a
great deal of his act.
First Lord. Sir, his wife some two months since fled
from his house: her pretence is a pilgrimage to
S. Jaques le Grand; which holy undertaking   50
with most austere sanctimony she accomplished;
and, there residing, the tenderness of her nature
became as a prey to her grief; in fine, made a groan
of her last breath, and now she sings in heaven.
Second Lord. How is this justified?   55
First Lord. The stronger part of it by her own letters,

35. *curiously*] F 1, 2; *seriously* F 3, 4.   56. *stronger*] *stranger* Collier (ed. 2) MS.

34. *judgments*] Ff. Pope reads judgment, a correction which is supported by S. Walker.
35. *curiously*] most carefully; or, perhaps, in a costly manner. See I. ii. 20, above.
35. *set*] like a counterfeit jewel.
43. *higher*] probably "further inland." See article, II. i. 12, 13.
51. *sanctimony*] here used in the old sense of sanctity (in *Othello* Shakespeare used it as we use it). Cf. "If vows be sanctimonies . . . if sanctimony be the gods' delight" (*Troilus and Cressida*, v. ii. 139).
55. *justified*] proved. Cf. "Say't, and justify it" (*Winter's Tale*, I. ii. 278). Also, "I could justify you traitors" (*Tempest*, v. i. 128).
56. *stronger part*] "main part"

which makes her story true, even to the point of
her death: her death itself, which could not be
her office to say is come, was faithfully confirmed
by the rector of the place. 60
Second Lord. Hath the count all this intelligence?
First Lord. Ay, and the particular confirmations, point
from point, to the full arming of the verity.
Second Lord. I am heartily sorry that he'll be glad of
this. 65
First Lord. How mightily sometimes we make us
comforts of our losses!
Second Lord. And how mightily some other times we
drown our gain in tears! The great dignity that
his valour hath here acquired for him shall at 70
home be encountered with a shame as ample.
First Lord. The web of our life is of a mingled yarn,
good and ill together: our virtues would be proud,
if our faults whipped them not; and our crimes
would despair, if they were not cherished by our 75
virtues.

Enter a Servant.

How now! where's your master?
Serv. He met the duke in the street, sir, of whom he
hath taken a solemn leave: his lordship will next
morning for France. The duke hath offered him 80
letters of commendations to the king.

62, 63. *point from point*] Ff, *from point to point* Hanmer, *point for point*
Capell. 69. *gain*] *gains* Camb. Edd. conj. 70. *acquired*] *requir'd* F 3, 4.

(Dyce). However, in his second edition,   60. *rector*] ruler, governor.
Dyce adopts Collier's correction "the   74. *our crimes* ...] we should despair
stranger part," which also appeared,   on account of our crimes, had we not
apparently through a misprint, in his   our virtues to console us.
first edition.

Second Lord. They shall be no more than needful
 there, if they were more than they can commend.
First Lord. They cannot be too sweet for the king's
 tartness. Here's his lordship now. 85

Enter BERTRAM.

How now, my lord! is't not after midnight?
Ber. I have to-night dispatched sixteen businesses, a
 month's length a-piece, by an abstract of success:
 I have congied with the duke, done my adieu with
 his nearest, buried a wife, mourned for her, writ 90
 to my lady mother I am returning, entertained
 my convoy; and between these main parcels of
 dispatch effected many nicer needs: the last was
 the greatest, but that I have not ended yet.
Second Lord. If the business be of any difficulty, and 95
 this morning your departure hence, it requires
 haste of your lordship.
Ber. I mean, the business is not ended, as fearing to
 hear of it hereafter. But shall we have this
 dialogue between the fool and the soldier? Come, 100
 bring forth this counterfeit module: has deceived
 me, like a double-meaning prophesier.

84. First Lord] Ber. F 1, 2; Cap. G. F 3, 4. In the Ff Bertram is made to enter after "can commend" (line 83). 89. *congied*] Ff; *conge'd* Capell. 93. *effected*] F 3, 4; *affected* F 1, 2. 101. *module*] Ff, *medal* Hanmer (Warburton), *model* Collier; *has*] F 2; *ha s* F 1; *'has* F 3, 4.

88. *an abstract of success*] "a string of successes," as we might say. "By a successful summary proceeding" (Schmidt). H. T., already quoted, gives "an abstract=an abridgment; success =succession; so that this phrase may mean in quick succession."

89. *congied with*] taken leave of (French, *congé*). It occurs as a noun, "congy." Shakespeare does not use the word elsewhere.

101. *module*] same as model. Cf. "All this thou seest is but a clod And module of confounded royalty" (*King John*, v. vii. 58).

102. *double-meaning*] zweideutig,

Second Lord. Bring him forth. [*Exeunt Soldiers.*
Has sat i' the stocks all night, poor gallant knave.
Ber. No matter; his heels have deserved it, in usurp- 105
ing his spurs so long. How does he carry himself?
First Lord. I have told your lordship already, the
stocks carry him. But to answer you as you
would be understood; he weeps like a wench
that had shed her milk: he hath confessed him- 110
self to Morgan, whom he supposes to be a friar,
from the time of his remembrance to this very
instant disaster of his setting i' the stocks; and
what think you he hath confessed?
Ber. Nothing of me, has a? 115
Second Lord. His confession is taken, and it shall be read
to his face: if your lordship be in 't, as I believe
you are, you must have the patience to hear it.

Re-enter Soldiers, with PAROLLES.

Ber. A plague upon him! muffled! he can say nothing
of me. 120
First Lord. Hush! hush! Hoodman comes! *Porto-tartarossa.*
First Sold. He calls for the tortures: what will you
say without 'em?

104. *Has*] *h'as* F 4; *ha's* F 1, 2, 3. Steevens proposes "he has" here and just above. But below we find (line 115) *ha's a* (F 1, 2, 3), *has a* (F 4), where it clearly means "has he"; hence "ha s" of F 1 probably stands for has—the he in both cases (101 and 104) having been dropped. 115. *has a?*] *ha's a* F 1, 2, 3; *has a* F 4; *has he* Rowe (ed. 2). 118. Re-enter . . .] Enter Parolles with his interpreter Ff. 121.] The Ff give the "Hush!" to Bertram (F 2, 3, 4, hush.).

undoubtedly a reference to the oracles which could be understood to mean yes or no.

121. *Hoodman comes*] an allusion to the game of blind man's buff, which was formerly called "Hod-man-blinde."

Par. I will confess what I know without constraint: 125
    if ye pinch me like a pasty, I can say no more.
First Sold. *Bosko chimurcho.*
Second Lord. *Boblibindo chicurmurco.*
First Sold. You are a merciful general. Our general
    bids you answer to what I shall ask you out of a 130
    note.
Par. And truly, as I hope to live.
First Sold. *First, demand of him how many horse the
    duke is strong.* What say you to that?
Par. Five or six thousand; but very weak and un- 135
    serviceable: the troops are all scattered, and the
    commanders very poor rogues, upon my reputa-
    tion and credit, and as I hope to live.
First Sold. Shall I set down your answer so?
Par. Do: I'll take the sacrament on't, how and 140
    which way you will.
Ber. All's one to him. What a past-saving slave
    is this!
First Lord. Y' are deceiv'd, my lord: this is Mon-
    sieur Parolles, the gallant militarist,—that was 145
    his own phrase,—that had the whole theoric of
    war in the knot of his scarf, and the practice in
    the chape of his dagger.

142. *All's . . . him. What*] Capell; *all's one to him.* Bert. *What* Ff.

145. *militarist*] This must literally be taken to be a phrase of his own coining. It is a parallel to his expression "facinerious" (II. iii. 31, above).
146. *theoric*] Cf. *Othello*, I. i. 24, and *Henry V.* I. i. 52. Hart in his note on the former passage says that it is one of the terms Ben Jonson ridicules, and it appears to have been introduced by Gabriel Harvey in his "Letters to Spenser," *Theoricks and Practicks*, about 1573.
148. *chape*] Schmidt defines it as "the metallic part at the end of the scabbard." *New Eng. Dict.*, "The metal plate or mounting of a scabbard or sheath; particularly that which covers the point."

Second Lord. I will never trust a man again for keeping his sword clean; nor believe he can have 150 every thing in him by wearing his apparel neatly.
First Sold. Well, that's set down.
Par. Five or six thousand horse, I said,—I will say true,—or thereabouts, set down, for I'll speak truth.
First Lord. He's very near the truth in this. 155
Ber. But I con him no thanks for't, in the nature he delivers it.
Par. Poor rogues, I pray you, say.
First Sold. Well, that's set down.
Par. I humbly thank you, sir. A truth's a truth; 160 the rogues are marvellous poor.
First Sold. *Demand of him, of what strength they are a-foot.* What say you to that?
Par. By my troth, sir, if I were to live this present hour, I will tell true. Let me see: Spurio, a 165 hundred and fifty; Sebastian, so many; Corambus, so many; Jaques, so many; Guiltian, Cosmo, Lodowick, and Gratii, two hundred fifty each; mine own company, Chitopher, Vaumond, Bentii, two hundred fifty each: so that the 170

149. Second Lord] Bertram (S. Walker conj.). 160, 161. *A truth's ... poor*] given to First Lord by Dyce (ed. 2) (S. Walker conj.). 164. *live*] *die* Dyce (ed. 2) (S. Walker conj.), *leave* Staunton conj., *live but this hour* Hanmer.

149.] In all probability S. Walker is right in conjecturing that this speech was meant for Bertram.

156. *con him no thanks*] "con" originally meant "know." Chaucer wrote, "Old wymen connen mochil thinge." It was used as in French, see Palsgrave (1530), 475-1, "I have conned hym good thanke: je luy ay sceu bon gré." Cf. also Wren, Serm. bef. King, 30, "I will kon them small thanks." (See also *New Eng. Dict.*)

164. *to live*] S. Walker is positive that this should be "die": to his note he adds *mira editorum ἀναισθησία*! I still prefer Tollet's explanation that "fear may be supposed to occasion Parolles' mistake; as poor frighted Scrub cries: 'Spare all I have, and take my life.'"

muster-file, rotten and sound, upon my life,
amounts not to fifteen thousand poll; half of
the which dare not shake the snow from off their
cassocks, lest they shake themselves to pieces.

Ber. What shall be done to him? 175

First Lord. Nothing, but let him have thanks. Demand of him my condition, and what credit I
have with the duke.

First Sold. Well, that's set down. *You shall demand of him, whether one Captain Dumain be i'* 180
*the camp, a Frenchman; what his reputation is
with the duke; what his valour, honesty, and
expertness in wars; or whether he thinks it were
not possible, with well-weighing sums of gold, to
corrupt him to a revolt.* What say you to this? 185
what do you know of it?

Par. I beseech you, let me answer to the particular
of the inter'gatories: demand them singly.

First Sold. Do you know this Captain Dumain?

Par. I know him: a was a botcher's prentice in Paris, 190
from whence he was whipped for getting the
shrieve's fool with child; a dumb innocent, that
could not say him nay.

172. *poll*] Theobald, *pole* Ff.   174. *lest*] F 4; *least* F 1, 2, 3.   187. *particular*] *particulars* Capell.   188. *inter'gatories*] F 1, 2, 3; *interrogatories*
F 4; *interrogatory* Capell.   193.] Johnson here adds *Dumain lifts his hand
in anger.*

174. *cassocks*] military cloaks. Delius quotes Glapthorne's *Hollander*, "Here, Sir, receive this military cassock, it has seen service."

184. well-weighing] has double meaning—weight and influence.

188. *inter'gatories*] Cf. "And charge us there upon inter'gatories" (*Merchant of Venice*, v. i. 298).

192. *shrieve's fool*] The word "fool" here means a woman who is an idiot and in the charge of a sheriff. "The custody of all 'ideots,' etc., possessed of landed property, belonged to the king,

Ber. Nay, by your leave, hold your hands; though I
    know his brains are forfeit to the next tile that falls. 195
First Sold. Well, is this captain in the Duke of
    Florence's camp?
Par. Upon my knowledge he is, and lousy.
First Lord. Nay, look not so upon me; we shall hear
    of your lordship anon. 200
First Sold. What is his reputation with the duke?
Par. The duke knows him for no other but a poor
    officer of mine, and writ to me this other day to
    turn him out o' the band: I think I have his
    letter in my pocket. 205
First Sold. Marry we'll search.
Par. In good sadness, I do not know: either it is
    there, or it is upon a file with the duke's other
    letters in my tent.
First Sold. Here 'tis; here's a paper; shall I read it 210
    to you?
Par. I do not know if it be it or no.
Ber. Our interpreter does it well.

---

200. *lordship*] Pope, *Lord* Ff.   204. *o' the*] *a' th* Ff.

who was entitled to the income of their lands, but obliged to find them with necessaries. This prerogative, when there was a large estate in the case, was generally granted to some court favourite, or other person who made suit for and had interest enough to obtain it, which was called 'begging a fool.' But when the land was of inconsiderable value, the 'natural' was maintained, out of the profits, by the 'sheriff,' who accounted for them to the crown. As for those unhappy creatures who had neither possessions nor relations, they seem to have been considered as a species of property, being sold or given with as little ceremony, treated as capriciously and very often, it is to be feared, left to perish as miserably, as cats or dogs" (Ritson).

195. *next tile*] a trite metaphor for sudden death. It is used by Lucian, Plutarch, and many others, including, as Rolfe mentions, Whitney, whose *Emblems* (1586) Shakespeare may have read.

198. *lousy*] low-born, despicable.

207. *In good sadness*] in earnest, "joking apart." Cf. "I think my leg would shew in a silken hose . . . In sadness I think it would" (*Every Man in his Humour*, I. ii.).

[SC. III.] THAT, ENDS WELL 127

First Lord. Excellently.
First Sold. *Dian, the count's a fool, and full of gold—* 215
Par. That is not the duke's letter, sir: that is an
 advertisement to a proper maid in Florence, one
 Diana, to take heed of the allurement of one Count
 Rousillon, a foolish idle boy, but for all that very
 ruttish. I pray you, sir, put it up again. 220
First Sold. Nay, I'll read it first, by your favour.
Par. My meaning in 't, I protest, was very honest
 in the behalf of the maid; for I knew the young
 count to be a dangerous and lascivious boy, who
 is a whale to virginity, and devours up all the 225
 fry it finds.
Ber. Damnable both-sides rogue!
First Sold. *When he swears oaths, bid him drop gold, and take it;*
 After he scores, he never pays the score:
 Half won is match well made; match, and well make it:
 He ne'er pays after-debts; take it before, 231
 And say a soldier, Dian, told thee this,
 Men are to mell with, boys are not to kiss;

215, 216.] Johnson supposes a line to be lost here. Steevens instead of "gold" conjectures "golden store" or "golden ore." Jackson reads "gold, I speak it," and lines 229-231 in this order: 230, 231, 229. Of course the fact that "gold" has nothing with which to rhyme may indicate that something is lost: but it seems just as likely that Shakespeare left it incomplete and began a fresh line 228. 230. well made] ill made Capell conj., half made Jackson conj.; match, and well] match. well and Hanmer, watch, and well Johnson conj., watch well and Rann; Johnson would read in this order: lines 230, 228, 229, 231; and well] an' we'll Steevens conj. 232, 233.] Capell would omit these lines as doubtful. 233. not to] but to Pope (Theobald).

220. *ruttish*] lustful (said of " Deere or Boares").
229. scores] takes (down a debt) hence incurs a debt. Cf. "Have you scored me?" (*Othello*, IV. i. 130).
230. Half won . . .] match made in business fashion is half won, so when you match, see that all is well arranged. Cf. *King John*, I. i. 174, "well won is still well shot . . ."
233. Men . . . kiss] The emphasis is probably on "men" and "boys," the words "mell" and "kiss" having much the same signification—that of

For count of this, the count's a fool, I know it,
Who pays before, but not when he does owe it. 235
Thine, as he vow'd to thee in thine ear,
                                           PAROLLES.

Ber. He shall be whipped through the army with
   this rhyme in's forehead.
Second Lord. This is your devoted friend, sir; the 240
   manifold linguist and the armipotent soldier.
Ber. I could endure any thing before but a cat, and
   now he's a cat to me.
First Sold. I perceive, sir, by our general's looks, we
   shall be fain to hang you.   245
Par. My life, sir, in any case! not that I am afraid
   to die; but that, my offences being many, I
   would repent out the remainder of nature. Let
   me live, sir, in a dungeon, i' the stocks, or anywhere, so I may live.   250
First Sold. We'll see what may be done, so you
   confess freely: therefore, once more to this
   Captain Dumain. You have answered to his
   reputation with the duke and to his valour: what
   is his honesty?   255

---

241. *armipotent*] Capell, *army-potent* Ff.   244. *our*] Capell; *your* F 1, 2; *the* F 3, 4.

dallying. "Mell" was frequently used in the sense of "meddling." Spenser wrote, "It fathers fits not with such things to mell." Dyce adopts the emendation "but to kiss."

234. *count of*] Cf. "no man counts of her beauty". (*Two Gentlemen of Verona*, II. i. 65).

241. *armipotent*] sometimes used as an epithet of God. Cf. "The armipotent Mars" (*Love's Labour's Lost*, v. ii. 650).

242. *a cat*] Bertram repeats the obloquy several times; it is, as Clarke points out, characteristically indicative of his bad-tempered vexation. Bertram is throughout revealed to us as a coward more base, perhaps, than Parolles. He lacks the faculty of "knowing what he is" which Parolles possesses. Besides, *noblesse oblige.*

248. *nature*] the "three score years and ten."

Par. He will steal, sir, an egg out of a cloister; for
rapes and ravishments he parallels Nessus; he
professes not keeping of oaths; in breaking 'em
he is stronger than Hercules; he will lie, sir,
with such volubility, that you would think truth 260
were a fool; drunkenness is his best virtue, for
he will be swine-drunk, and in his sleep he does
little harm, save to his bed-clothes about him;
but they know his conditions, and lay him in
straw. I have but little more to say, sir, of his 265
honesty: he has every thing that an honest man
should not have; what an honest man should
have, he has nothing.
First Lord. I begin to love him for this.
Ber. For this description of thine honesty? A pox 270
upon him for me! he is more and more a cat.
First Sold. What say you to his expertness in war?
Par. Faith, sir, has led the drum before the English
tragedians,—to belie him I will not,—and more
of his soldiership I know not; except, in that 275
country he had the honour to be the officer at a
place there called Mile-end, to instruct for the

256. *egg*] *Ag.* (*i.e.* Agnes) Becket conj.   263, 264. *bed-clothes . . . they*]
bed-clothes; but they about him Watkiss Lloyd conj.   273. *has*] *ha's* Ff.

256. *egg . . . cloister*] Used generally to be understood to mean that he would steal the most worthless thing from a holy place. It may refer to the old custom of blessing eggs ("Bless, O Lord, we beseech Thee, this Thy creature of eggs . . .") to which Falstaff referred when he said, "Thou hast not so much grace in thee, as to bless thee an egg." Someone suggested to Mr. Thiselton that we should read "clyster" (cleister). He understands that an egg is an ingredient in such preparations, and thinks that such "a masterpiece of nasty greed" would be quite in keeping with the Parolles's humour. It is a brilliant conjecture.

277. *Mile-end*] the proverbial drill ground. Cf. "Your devices in the war (are) not like those a man . . . sees at Mile End" (Ben Jonson, *Every Man in his Humour*, IV. ii.).

9

doubling of files: I would do the man what honour
I can, but of this I am not certain.
First Lord. He hath out-villained villany so far that 280
the rarity redeems him.
Ber. A pox on him! he's a cat still.
First Sold. His qualities being at this poor price, I
need not to ask you if gold will corrupt him to
revolt. 285
Par. Sir, for a cardecue he will sell the fee-simple of
his salvation, the inheritance of it; and cut the
entail from all remainders, and a perpetual
succession for it perpetually.
First Sold. What's his brother, the other Captain 290
Dumain?
Second Lord. Why does he ask him of me?
First Sold. What's he?
Par. E'en a crow o' the same nest; not altogether so
great as the first in goodness, but greater a great 295
deal in evil. He excels his brother for a coward,
yet his brother is reputed one of the best that is.
In a retreat he outruns any lackey; marry, in
coming on he has the cramp.

280. *out-villained*] *out-villanied* S. Walker conj.   286. *cardecue*] F 2, 3, 4;
cardecue F 1.   289. *for it*] *in it* Hanmer.

280. *out-villained villany*] the obvious parallel is "out-herod Herod."
286. *cardecue*] eightpence.
286. *fee-simple*] "tenant in fee-simple ... is he which hath lands or tenements to hold to him and to his heir for ever (Littleton); an estate in remainder is the residue of an estate, in land depending upon a particular estate and created together with the same. A particular estate is that which is derived from a general and greater estate (Wood)."—Rushton.
292. *Why ... me?*] Johnson remarks that "every man is, on such occasions, more willing to hear his neighbours' character than his own."
298. *lackey*] a footman who "ran." The *New Eng. Dict.* gives an instance from *The Times Whistle*, iii. 106, "lackeys before her chariot run."

First Sold. If your life be saved, will you undertake to 300
  betray the Florentine?
Par. Ay, and the captain of his horse, Count Rousillon.
First Sold. I'll whisper with the general, and know
  his pleasure.
Par. [*Aside.*] I'll no more drumming; a plague of all 305
  drums! Only to seem to deserve well, and to
  beguile the supposition of that lascivious young
  boy the count, have I run into this danger. Yet
  who would have suspected an ambush where I
  was taken? 310
First Sold. There is no remedy, sir, but you must
  die. The general says, you that have so
  traitorously discovered the secrets of your army,
  and made such pestiferous reports of men very
  nobly held, can serve the world for no honest 315
  use; therefore you must die. Come, headsman,
  off with his head.
Par. O Lord, sir, let me live, or let me see my death!
First Sold. That shall you, and take your leave of all
  your friends. [*Unmuffling him.* 320
  So, look about you: know you any here?
Ber. Good morrow, noble captain.
Second Lord. God bless you, Captain Parolles.
First Lord. God save you, noble captain.
Second Lord. Captain, what greeting will you to my 325
  Lord Lafeu? I am for France.
First Lord. Good captain, will you give me a copy of
  the sonnet you writ to Diana in behalf of the

---

305. [Aside] Rowe (ed. 2), omitted Ff. 320. Unmuffling him] Steevens, omitted Ff. 328. *the sonnet*] F 1, 2; *the same sonnet* F 3, 4.

Count Rousillon? an I were not a very coward
I'd compel it of you; but fare you well. 330
[Exeunt Bertram and Lords.

First Sold. You are undone, captain; all but your
scarf; that has a knot on 't yet.

Par. Who cannot be crushed with a plot?

First Sold. If you could find out a country where but
women were that had received so much shame, 335
you might begin an impudent nation. Fare ye
well, sir; I am for France too: we shall speak of
you there. *[Exit.*

Par. Yet am I thankful: if my heart were great
'Twould burst at this. Captain I'll be no more; 340
But I will eat and drink, and sleep as soft
As captain shall: simply the thing I am
Shall make me live. Who knows himself a braggart,
Let him fear this; for it will come to pass
That every braggart shall be found an ass. 345
Rust, sword! cool, blushes! and, Parolles, live
Safest in shame! being fool'd, by foolery thrive!
There's place and means for every man alive.
I'll after them. *[Exit*

329. *an*] Capell, *and* Ff.

345.] S. Walker says: "There is perhaps a line lost after 'found an ass.' Something seems to be wanting; *live—thrive*, too, is a suspicious rhyme for Shakespeare's age; triplets are very rare in him, and occur only, I think, under special circumstances. Perhaps, however, a rhyme is not wanted here."

348. *There's place . . .*] A line characteristic of Shakespeare's genius. He seems to have had sympathy with this miserable "thing" simply because it was a fellow-man.

SCENE IV.—*Florence. A Room in the Widow's House.*

Enter HELENA, *Widow, and* DIANA.

Hel. That you may well perceive I have not wrong'd you,
One of the greatest in the Christian world
Shall be my surety; 'fore whose throne 'tis needful,
Ere I can perfect mine intents, to kneel.
Time was, I did him a desired office, 5
Dear almost as his life; which gratitude
Through flinty Tartar's bosom would peep forth,
And answer, thanks. I duly am inform'd
His grace is at Marsellis; to which place
We have convenient convoy. You must know, 10
I am supposed dead: the army breaking,
My husband hies him home; where, heaven aiding,
And by the leave of my good lord the king,
We'll be before our welcome.

Wid. Gentle madam,
You never had a servant to whose trust 15
Your business was more welcome.

Hel. Nor you, mistress,
Ever a friend whose thoughts more truly labour
To recompense your love. Doubt not but heaven
Hath brought me up to be your daughter's dower,
As it hath fated her to be my motive 20

---

3. *'fore*] *for* F 1.   9. *Marsellis*] F 2, 3; *Marcellæ* F 1; *Marselis* F 4.   16. *you,*] Rowe; *you* F 4; *your* F 1, 2, 3.

9. *Marsellis*] Marseilles, pronounced as a trisyllable.
10. *convoy*] means of conveyance. Cf. "As the winds give benefit and convoy is assistant, let me hear from you" (*Hamlet*, I. iii. 3).
11. *breaking*] disbanding.
20. *motive*] whatever makes a thing

And helper to a husband. But, O strange men!
That can such sweet use make of what they hate,
When saucy trusting of the cozen'd thoughts
Defiles the pitchy night: so lust doth play
With what it loathes for that which is away.   25
But more of this hereafter. You, Diana,
Under my poor instructions yet must suffer
Something in my behalf.

Dia.   Let death and honesty
Go with your impositions, I am yours
Upon your will to suffer.

Hel.   Yet, I pray you: 30
But with the word the time will bring on summer,
When briars shall have leaves as well as thorns,
And be as sweet as sharp. We must away;
Our waggon is prepar'd, and time revives us:
All's well that ends well: still the fine's the crown; 35
Whate'er the course, the end is the renown.

                                                         [*Exeunt.*

35. *the fine's*] Theobald; *the fine* F 1; *that fines* F 2, 3; *that finds* F 4.

move, the cause of motion. Cf. "The slavish motive of recanting fear" (=tongue) (*Richard II.* I. i. 193); also "all impediments in fancy's course are motives of more fancy" (v. iii. 214, below).

23. *saucy trusting*] wantonly giving the rein to or entertaining. Goneril (*King Lear*, I. iv. 350) says in answer to Albany's "you may fear too far"— "Safer than trust too far. Let me still take away the harms I fear." Also, "as to remit Their saucy sweetness, that do coin heaven's image In stamps that are forbid" (*Measure for Measure*, II. iv. 45).

30. *Yet*] as in "yet forty days, and Nineveh shall be overthrown" (Jonah iii. 4).

31. *with the word*] obscure. Perhaps the drift of the meaning is "I must still pray you 'upon my will to suffer': but it is with my word, my promise, that time will turn the bitter into sweet."

34. *revives us*] Cf. "that our God may lighten our eyes, and give us a little reviving in our bondage" (Ezra ix. 8).

35. *the fine*] "Finis coronat opus," as Boswell says. "La fin couronne les œuvres" (*2 Henry VI.* v. ii. 28). We still use the word in the phrase "in fine."

SCENE V.—*Rousillon. A Room in the Countess's Palace.*

Enter COUNTESS, LAFEU, *and Clown.*

Laf. No, no, no; your son was misled with a snipt-taffeta fellow there, whose villanous saffron would have made all the unbaked and doughy youth of a nation in his colour: your daughter-in-law had been alive at this hour, and your son 5 here at home, more advanced by the king than by that red-tailed humble-bee I speak of.

Count. I would I had not known him; it was the death of the most virtuous gentlewoman that ever nature had praise for creating. If she had partaken of my 10 flesh, and cost me the dearest groans of a mother, I could not have owed her a more rooted love.

Laf. 'Twas a good lady, 'twas a good lady: we may pick a thousand salads ere we light on such another herb. 15

Clo. Indeed, sir, she was the sweet-marjoram of the salad, or rather the herb of grace.

Laf. They are not herbs, you knave; they are nose-herbs.

Clo. I am no great Nebuchadnezzar, sir; I have not 20 much skill in grass.

---

8. *I had*] *he had* Hanmer (Theobald conj.), Mason and Dyce. 14. *salads*] Reed, *sallets* Ff (as also line 17). 18. *herbs*] *sallet-herbs* Rowe, *pot-hearbes* Collier MS. 21. *grass*] Rowe, *grace* Ff.

2. *villanous saffron*] There is some reference to the favourite yellow dye used for various purposes.
11. *dearest*] direst, as frequently.
17. *herb of grace*] rue, so called "because holy water was sprinkled with it" (Johnson).
18, 19. *nose-herbs*] scented flowers (cf. nosegay).

Laf. Whether dost thou profess thyself, a knave or a
    fool?
Clo. A fool, sir, at a woman's service, and a knave at
    a man's. 25
Laf. Your distinction?
Clo. I would cozen the man of his wife, and do his
    service.
Laf. So you were a knave at his service, indeed.
Clo. And I would give his wife my bauble, sir, to do 30
    her service.
Laf. I will subscribe for thee, thou art both knave and
    fool.
Clo. At your service.
Laf. No, no, no. 35
Clo. Why, sir, if I cannot serve you, I can serve as
    great a prince as you are.
Laf. Who's that? a Frenchman?
Clo. Faith, sir, a' has an English name; but his fisnomy
    is more hotter in France than there. 40
Laf. What prince is that?
Clo. The black prince, sir; *alias*, the prince of dark-
    ness; *alias*, the devil.
Laf. Hold thee, there's my purse. I give thee not

39. *name*] Rowe; *maine* F 1, 2; *main* F 3; *mean* F 4; *mien* Anon. conj.
40. *hotter*] *honour'd* Hanmer (Warburton).

30. *bauble*] the stick of a court fool; the word was frequently used equivocally. (See *Romeo and Juliet*, II. iv. 97.)
39. *an English name*] namely, the Black Prince. The "authentic" versions read "maine." Some editors have taken this to refer to the hairiness of "Old Harry"; but they do not explain why the hair should be English.
40. *more hotter*] Warburton's emendation "honour'd" for "hotter" has been adopted by many editors; but there is little reason to suppose that Shakespeare did not write "more hotter."

this to suggest thee from thy master thou talkest 45
of: serve him still.

Clo. I am a woodland fellow, sir, that always loved a
great fire; and the master I speak of ever keeps
a good fire. But, sure, he is the prince of the
world; let his nobility remain in's court. I am 50
for the house with the narrow gate, which I take
to be too little for pomp to enter: some that
humble themselves may; but the many will be
too chill and tender, and they'll be for the flowery
way that leads to the broad gate and the great fire. 55

Laf. Go thy ways, I begin to be aweary of thee; and
I tell thee so before, because I would not fall out
with thee. Go thy ways: let my horses be well
looked to, without any tricks.

Clo. If I put any tricks upon 'em, sir, they shall be 60
jades' tricks, which are their own right by the law
of nature. [*Exit*

Laf. A shrewd knave and an unhappy.

---

45. *suggest*] *seduce* Rowe (ed. 2).   49. *sure*] *since* Hanmer, *for* Capell.

45. *suggest thee*] tempt thee to leave.
54. *too chill*] too hesitating, too lukewarm.
54, 55. *flowery way*] Steevens aptly quotes "the primrose way to the everlasting bonfire."
59. *tricks*] a reference to the greasing of horses' teeth to prevent their eating the forage the ostler thought well to appropriate.
63. *shrewd*] mischievous. "A shrewd unhappy gallows" (*Love's Labour's Lost*, V. ii. 12). "unhappy" =unlucky. Mr. Craig quotes from Holland's *Pliny* (*Nat. Hist.*, Bk. XIX. chap. VI. pt. ii. p. 22, K. ed., 1634):

"There is a kind of garlicke growing wilde in the fieldes . . . which being boiled that it should not grow, they commonly throw forth in cornfields for the shrewd, unhappy foules which lie upon the land and eat up the seed new sown; for presently as any of these birds taste thereof they will be drunk." In this instance "unhappy" is more likely to mean "mischievous" than "unlucky." Cf. *Much Ado*, II. i. 361, "She hath often dreamed of unhappiness, and waked herself with laughing." The construction "and an unhappy" is not unusual. Delius quotes a parallel from Paynter, "A fair maid and a comely."

Count. So he is. My lord that's gone made himself
much sport out of him: by his authority he re- 65
mains here, which he thinks is a patent for his
sauciness; and, indeed, he has no pace, but runs
where he will.

Laf. I like him well; 'tis not amiss. And I was about
to tell you, since I heard of the good lady's death, 70
and that my lord your son was upon his return
home, I moved the king my master to speak in
the behalf of my daughter; which, in the minority
of them both, his majesty, out of a self-gracious
remembrance, did first propose. His highness 75
hath promised me to do it; and to stop up the
displeasure he hath conceived against your son,
there is no fitter matter. How does your ladyship like it?

Count. With very much content, my lord; and I wish 80
it happily effected.

Laf. His highness comes post from Marsellis, of as
able body as when he numbered thirty: a will be
here to-morrow, or I am deceived by him that in
such intelligence hath seldom failed. 85

Count. It rejoices me, that I hope I shall see him ere I
die. I have letters that my son will he here to-

---

67. *pace*] *place* Hanmer, *pause* W. J. Craig conj.   75. *propose*] *purpose* S.
Walker conj.   82. *Marsellis*] F 2; *Marcellus* F 1; *Marselles* F 3, 4.   86.
It] *Ir* F 1, *I* F 2.

---

67. *pace*] Schmidt understands this to mean "he observes no rule, pays no regard to form." The metaphor is probably taken from horse-breaking and training — the clown has no restraint laid on him.

74. *self-gracious*] gracious to himself. Cf. "Infusing him with self and vain conceit" (*Richard II.* III. ii. 166). Also, "Who by self and violent hands took off her life" (*Macbeth*, v. viii. 70).

night: I shall beseech your lordship to remain
with me till they meet together.

Laf. Madam, I was thinking with what manners I 90
might safely be admitted.

Count. You need but plead your honourable privilege.

Laf. Lady, of that I have made a bold charter; but
I thank my God it holds yet.

Re-enter Clown.

Clo. O madam! yonder's my lord your son with a 95
patch of velvet on's face: whether there be a
scar under 't or no, the velvet knows; but 'tis a
goodly patch of velvet. His left cheek is a cheek
of two pile and a half, but his right cheek is worn
bare. 100

Laf. A scar nobly got, or a noble scar, is a good
livery of honour; so belike is that.

Clo. But it is your carbonadoed face.

Laf. Let us go see your son, I pray you: I long to
talk with the young noble soldier. 105

Clo. Faith, there's a dozen of 'em, with delicate fine
hats and most courteous feathers, which bow the
head and nod at every man. [*Exeunt.*

103. *carbonadoed*] Theobald, *carbinado'd* Ff.

98.] Cf. *Measure for Measure*, I. ii., "... And thou the velvet; thou art good velvet; thou 'rt a three piled piece, I warrant thee: I had as lief be a list of an English kersey as be piled, as thou art piled for a French velvet."

101.] Malone says that it is more likely that the countess should have spoken thus favourably of Bertram than Lafeu. But Lafeu was hoping to become his father-in-law.

103. *carbonadoed face*] "A carbonado is a piece of meat cut so as to be cooked on a gridiron. The word is still used in France" (Schmidt). Cf. *King Lear*, II. ii. 41, "I'll carbonado your shanks for you." In his note on this passage, Mr. Craig quotes Cotgrave: "*Carbonade*, a carbonadoe, a rasher on the coals; also a flash over the face which fetcheth the flesh with it."

ACT V

SCENE I.—*Marseilles. A Street.*

Enter HELENA, WIDOW, *and* DIANA, *with two Attendants*.

Hel. But this exceeding posting day and night,
 Must wear your spirits low; we cannot help it:
 But since you have made the days and nights as one,
 To wear your gentle limbs in my affairs,
 Be bold you do so grow in my requital 5
 As nothing can unroot you. In happy time;

Enter a gentle Astringer.

This man may help me to his majesty's ear,
 If he would spend his power. God save you, sir.
Gent. And you.
Hel. Sir, I have seen you in the court of France. 10
Gent. I have been sometimes there.
Hel. I do presume, sir, that you are not fallen
 From the report that goes upon your goodness;
 And therefore, goaded with most sharp occasions,

Marseilles. A Street.] Capell. The Court of France. Pope. 6. a gentle Astringer] F 1; Enter a gentle Astranger F 2; Enter a gentleman a stranger F 3, 4.

5. *Be bold*] be sure. Cf. "I would I were so sure To win the king as I am bold her honour Will remain hers" (*Cymbeline*, II. iv, 2).

6. Enter a gentle Astringer] "An ostringer or astringer is a falconer, and such a character is probably to be met with about a court which was famous for the love of that diversion . . .

A 'gentle astringer' is a 'gentleman falconer.' . . . Cowell in his *Law Dict.* says, 'We usually call a falconer, who keeps that kind of hawk, an austringer'" (Steevens). The word "astringer" may have been added to the MS. by the manager of the theatre merely to indicate the costume.

sc. I.] THAT ENDS WELL   141

  Which lay nice manners by, I put you to 15
  The use of your own virtues, for the which
  I shall continue thankful.
Gent.   What's your will?
Hel. That it will please you
  To give this poor petition to the king,
  And aid me with that store of power you have 20
  To come into his presence.
Gent. The king's not here.
Hel.   Not here, sir!
Gent.   Not, indeed:
  He hence remov'd last night, and with more haste
  Than is his use.
Wid.   Lord, how we lose our pains!
Hel. All's well that ends well yet, 25
  Though time seem so adverse and means unfit.
  I do beseech you, whither is he gone?
Gent. Marry, as I take it, to Rousillon;
  Whither I am going.
Hel.   I do beseech you, sir,
  Since you are like to see the king before me, 30
  Commend the paper to his gracious hand;
  Which I presume shall render you no blame
  But rather make you thank your pains for it.
  I will come after you with what good speed
  Our means will make us means.
Gent.   This I'll do for you 35
Hel. And you shall find yourself to be well thank'd,

---

16. *virtues*] *virtue* S. Walker conj. 35. *make us means.*] *make us.* Anon. conj. 36–38.] Prose in Ff; verse first by Pope.

23. *remov'd*] the word was used as a rule for the movements of monarchs.

Whate'er falls more. We must to horse again:
Go, go, provide. [*Exeunt.*

SCENE II.—*Rousillon. The inner Court of the Countess's Palace.*

Enter Clown and PAROLLES.

Par. Good Mr. Lavache, give my Lord Lafeu this letter.
I have ere now, sir, been better known to you,
when I have held familiarity with fresher clothes;
but I am now, sir, muddied in fortune's mood, and
smell somewhat strong of her strong displeasure. 5

Clo. Truly, fortune's displeasure is but sluttish if it
smell so strongly as thou speakest of: I will
henceforth eat no fish of fortune's buttering.
Prithee, allow the wind.

Par. Nay, you need not to stop your nose, sir: I 10
spake but by a metaphor.

4. *mood*] *moat* Theobald. "Theobald altered 'mood' to 'moat'; but a quibble between 'mood' and 'mud' is intended here,—the words having been formerly pronounced nearly alike" (Dyce). 11. *spake*] F 1; *speake* F 2; *speak* F 3, 4.

37. *falls*] befalls. Cf. v. iii. 121, below.

Scene II.

1. *Lavache*] If Parolles's name is taken from the French, it is just as probable that "Lavatch," which we have in the Ff, is the English spelling of La Vache. Clarke derives it from "lavage." Tollet thinks Shakespeare may have made some punning allusion to the name of the actor who played the part, namely, either Richard Cowley or John Lowine.

4. *mood*] This is the Ff reading, and no comment would have been required had not Theobald hit upon the idea of changing it to "moat," for which many reasons can be urged. Steevens goes so far as to call it "one of the luckiest ever produced." Be that as it may, it is surely best policy to retain the reading of the only "authentic" version we possess. Shakespeare often uses the word mood to imply displeasure, so that there is little reason for supposing that he did not write "muddied in fortune's mood" if he wrote "I smell of her strong displeasure." The two sentences are parallel.

Clo. Indeed, sir, if your metaphor stink, I will stop
my nose; or against any man's metaphor.
Prithee, get thee further.
Par. Pray you, sir, deliver me this paper. 15
Clo. Foh! prithee, stand away: a paper from fortune's close-stool to give to a nobleman! Look,
here he comes himself.

Enter LAFEU.

Here is a pur of fortune's, sir, or of fortune's cat,
but not a musk-cat, that has fallen into the un- 20
clean fishpond of her displeasure, and, as he says,
is muddied withal. Pray you, sir, use the carp
as you may, for he looks like a poor, decayed,
ingenious, foolish, rascally knave. I do pity his
distress in my similes of comfort, and leave him 25
to your lordship. [*Exit.*
Par. My lord, I am a man whom fortune hath cruelly
scratched.
Laf. And what would you have me to do? 'Tis too

19. *pur*] F 4; *purre* F 1, 2, 3; *puss* Mason conj.; *or of fortune's cat*] *or fortune's cat* Warburton. 20. *musk-cat*] Theobald, *muscat* Ff, *mouse-cat* Anon. conj. 25. *similes*] Theobald (Warburton), *smiles* Ff. 26. Exit] Capell, omitted Ff.

24. *ingenious*] probably "not in-genious." Ingenious is used by Shake-speare to mean intellectually gifted, as in "bold, quick, ingenious, forward, capable" (*Richard III.* III. i. 155). The word here seems to be used as if there were an adjective "genious" with a negative prefix "in." Cf. "ingag'd," v. iii. 96, below. The *New Eng. Dict.* quotes, 1621, Brathwait, *Nat. Emb. Beggarie* (1877), 43, "Sprong of ingenerous bloud"; the word "ingenious," as used in this instance, may be a corruption of "ingenerous."

25. *similes*] Steevens quotes an entry on the books of the Stationers' Company (1595): "A booke of verie pythie similies, comfortable and pro-fitable for all men to read." He adds that the misprint "smiles" for "similies" occurs in the old copies of *1 Henry IV.* I. ii. 89, where instead of "unsavoury similies" we read "un-savoury smiles."

late to pare her nails now. Wherein, have you 30
played the knave with fortune that she should
scratch you, who of herself is a good lady, and
would not have knaves thrive long under her?
There's a cardecue for you. Let the justices
make you and fortune friends; I am for other 35
business.

Par. I beseech your honour to hear me one single
word.

Laf. You beg a single penny more: come, you shall
ha't; save your word. 40

Par. My name, my good lord, is Parolles.

Laf. You beg more than one word then. Cox my
passion! give me your hand. How does your
drum?

Par. O my good lord! you were the first that found me. 45

Laf. Was I, in sooth? and I was the first that lost
thee.

Par. It lies in you, my lord, to bring me in some
grace, for you did bring me out.

Laf. Out upon thee, knave! dost thou put upon me 50
at once both the office of God and the devil?
One brings thee in grace and the other brings
thee out. [*Trumpets sound.*

33. *under her?*] F 2, 3, 4; *under?* F 1. 42. *one word*] F 3, 4; *word* F 1, 2; *a word* Collier (Egerton MS.). 51. *devil?*] Pope, *diuel:* F 1. 53. Trumpets sound] Theobald, omitted Ff.

34. *the justices*] "The reference is to the Poor Law, by which Justices of the Peace had to grant a pauper's maintenance" (H. T.).

42. *word*] Evidently a play on the name Parolles. Malone thinks that one was unnecessarily added by the editor of F 3, a quibble being intended on the word Parolles. Cf., however, what Parolles says in line 37, "hear me one single word" (Dr. Proescholdt).

42, 43. *Cox my passion*] God's (my) passion; probably a corruption of "God's passion." Cf. "Cock's passion, silence!" (*Taming of the Shrew,* IV. i. 121).

sc. III.] THAT ENDS WELL 145

> The king's coming; I know by his trumpets.
> Sirrah, inquire further after me; I had talk of 55
> you last night: though you are a fool and a
> knave, you shall eat: go to, follow.
>
> *Par.* I praise God for you. [*Exeunt.*

SCENE III.—*The Same. A Room in the
Countess's Palace.*

Flourish. Enter KING, COUNTESS, LAFEU,
Lords, Gentlemen, Guards, etc.

King. We lost a jewel of her, and our esteem
    Was made much poorer by it: but your son,
    As mad in folly, lack'd the sense to know
    Her estimation home.
Count.   'Tis past, my liege;
    And I beseech your majesty to make it 5
    Natural rebellion, done i' the blaze of youth;
    When oil and fire, too strong for reason's force,
    O'erbears it and burns on.

6. *blaze*] Warburton (Theobald conj.), *blade* Ff, *blood* Perring conj.

1. *esteem*] In *Troilus and Cressida* Shakespeare uses the phrase "most dear in the esteem and poor in worth," which illustrates exactly the meaning of "esteem," namely, the supposed worth as opposed to the real worth. So "esteem" may mean self-esteem or else the value at which others esteem us; it therefore means here either "we are less rich in self-esteem," or "we are less rich in things that we esteem" since she is gone. Cf. inscription on Molière's bust: "*Rien ne manque à sa gloire, il manquait à la nôtre.*"

3. *As*] as if.
4. *home*] to know home is to know very completely. Cf. "I cannot speak him home" (*Coriolanus*, II. ii. 107); "tax him home" (*Hamlet*, III. iii. 29).
6. *blaze*] The Ff read "blade." The word blade is nowhere else used by Shakespeare in such a context (though in a similar metaphor sometimes); nor does it seem in any way an appropriate word to precede such a simile as "when oil and fire o'erbears reason and burns on."

10

King.   My honour'd lady,
   I have forgiven and forgotten all,
   Though my revenges were high bent upon him,   10
   And watch'd the time to shoot.
Laf.   This I must say,—
   But first I beg my pardon,—the young lord
   Did to his majesty, his mother, and his lady,
   Offence of mighty note, but to himself
   The greatest wrong of all: he lost a wife   15
   Whose beauty did astonish the survey
   Of richest eyes, whose words all ears took captive,
   Whose dear perfection hearts that scorn'd to serve
   Humbly call'd mistress.
King.   Praising what is lost
   Makes the remembrance dear. Well, call him
      hither;   20
   We are reconcil'd, and the first view shall kill
   All repetition. Let him not ask our pardon:
   The nature of his great offence is dead,
   And deeper than oblivion we do bury
   The incensing relics of it: let him approach,   25
   A stranger, no offender; and inform him
   So 'tis our will he should.
Gent.   I shall, my liege.   [*Exit.*
King. What says he to your daughter? have you spoke?
Laf. All that he is hath reference to your highness.

24. *we do*] *do we* Reed.   28. *What . . . spoke?*] Two lines in Ff, ending "daughter," . . . "spoke?"

10. *high bent*] a metaphor from archery.
17. *richest eyes*] "to have seen much . . . is to have rich eyes" (*As You Like It*, IV. i. 24).
29. *reference*] Cf. "Many things having reference to one consent, may work contrariously" (*Henry V.* I. ii. 205).

King. Then shall we have a match. I've letters sent
    me   30
    That sets him high in fame.

              Enter BERTRAM.

Laf.   He looks well on 't.
King. I 'm not a day of season,
    For thou mayst see a sunshine and a hail
    In me at once; but to the brightest beams
    Distracted clouds give way: so stand thou forth; 35
    The time is fair again.
Ber.   My high-repented blames,
    Dear sovereign, pardon to me.
King.   All is whole;
    Not one word more of the consumed time.
    Let 's take the instant by the forward top,
    For we are old, and on our quick'st decrees   40
    The inaudible and noiseless foot of time,
    Steals ere we can effect them. You remember
    The daughter of this lord?
Ber. Admiringly, my liege. At first
    I stuck my choice upon her, ere my heart   45
    Durst make too bold a herald of my tongue,
    Where the impression of mine eye infixing,

30, 31.] Prose in Ff; verse first by Pope.   32. *season*] *summer* Clark MS., *seasonable weather* Keightley conj.   44. *Admiringly, my liege.*] Rowe; *Admiringly my liege*, F 1, 2; *Admiringly, my liege,* F 3, 4.   46.] After this line Keightley thinks that a line may be lost, conveying the meaning, "Another object met my wandering fancy."

    30. *letters*] singular. Cf. IV. v. 87, above.
    32. *not . . . season*] I am a day out of season.
    45. *stuck . . . upon*] "Stick" was used by Shakespeare not only in the sense which we understand now ("a saw a flea stuck upon Bardolph's nose"), but also in a more dignified sense. "Honour stuck upon him as the sun in the grey vault of heaven" (*2 Henry IV*. II. iii. 18).

Contempt his scornful perspective did lend me,
Which warp'd the line of every other favour;
Scorn'd a fair colour, or express'd it stolen;   50
Extended or contracted all proportions
To a most hideous object: thence it came
That she, whom all men prais'd, and whom myself,
Since I have lost, have lov'd, was in mine eye
The dust that did offend it.

King.   Well excus'd: 55
That thou didst love her, strikes some scores away
From the great compt. But love, that comes too late,
Like a remorseful pardon slowly carried,
To the great sender turns a sour offence,
Crying, "That's good that's gone." Our rash faults
Make trivial price of serious things we have,   61
Not knowing them until we know their grave:
Oft our displeasures, to ourselves unjust,
Destroy our friends and after weep their dust:
Our own love waking cries to see what's done,   65
While shameful hate sleeps out the afternoon.

49. *warp'd*] *warpt* F 1, 2; *wrapt* F 3, 4.   50. *Scorn'd*] *Scorch'd* Hanmer (Warburton), *Scors'd* Becket conj.   58, 59. *carried, . . . sender*] Theobald, *carried . . . sender*, Ff.   61. *trivial*] F 1, 2; *triall* F 3; *trial* F 4.   65, 66.] Johnson considered these two lines spurious.   66. *shameful hate*] *shame full late* Globe edition (W. G. C., *Fraser Mag.* conj.).

48. *perspective*] The old word for telescope is here used to mean a special kind of glass. "Perspectives, which rightly gazed upon, show nothing but confusion, eyed awry distinguish form" (*Richard II.* II. ii. 18). Cf. also, 1615, John Stephens, *Satyrical Essays*, character xvii. p. 301, "My mistresse is my perspective glasse, through which I view the world's vanity" (*Trans. New Shak. Soc.*).

57. *compt*] reckoning, as in "When we shall meet at compt" (*Othello*, V. ii. 273), where it means the final reckoning.

60. *rash faults*] Lettsom would read "rasher faults."

66.] This line is by many editors supposed to be corrupt. Sleep out the afternoon probably means to sleep all the afternoon, having completed one's work in the morning. Hate has done its best and now sleeps at ease. Cf. "Thou hast not youth nor age; But,

Be this sweet Helen's knell, and now forget her.
Send forth your amorous token for fair Maudlin:
The main consents are had; and here we'll stay
To see our widower's second marriage-day. 70
Count. Which better than the first, O dear heaven, bless!
Or, ere they meet, in me, O nature, cesse!
Laf. Come on, my son, in whom my house's name
Must be digested, give a favour from you
To sparkle in the spirits of my daughter, 75
That she may quickly come.

[*Bertram gives a ring.*

By my old beard,
And every hair that's on 't, Helen, that's dead,
Was a sweet creature; such a ring as this,
The last that e'er I took her leave at court,
I saw upon her finger.

---

71. Count] Theobald, continued to king in Ff. 72. *meet*,] Rowe; no comma in Ff. 79. *that e'er I*] *that ere I* Ff.

---

as it were, an after-dinner's sleep, Dreaming on both . . ." (*Measure for Measure*, III. i. 32).

68. *Maudlin*] Magdalen. It may be only a coincidence that the heroine of this play has Shakespeare's favourite name (if we may judge by the frequent use), whereas her substitute is given a name apparently distasteful to him, for we only come across it once again, in the *Comedy of Errors*, as a servant's name.

71, 72. *Which . . . cesse!*] The Ff give this speech to the king. The mistake is palpable.

72. *cesse*] old spelling, retained for the sake of the rhyme.

73. *son*] son-in-law.

74. *digested*] amalgamated. Cf. "With my two daughters' dowers digest this third" (*King Lear*, I. i. 130).

79. *The last*] the last time (see Abbott, § 48); "her" seems to be used for "of her," "at her hands," *i.e.* I bade her farewell (Abbott, § 220) [Prof. Proescholdt]. Lettsom observes, "The last that" cannot possibly mean "the last time that": if it means anything, he says, it must mean "the last ring that." "Nor is it English to say 'take a person's leave' for 'take leave of a person.'" He would therefore read "The last eve, ere she took her leave at court." It seems rather beside the mark to discuss the "English." Shakespeare used the language very much as he pleased, as poor Johnson so often discovered. Taking "the last" to mean "the last time" makes the passage quite clear, and I think that suffices.

Ber.   Hers it was not.   80
King. Now, pray you, let me see it; for mine eye,
    While I was speaking, oft was fasten'd to't.
    This ring was mine; and, when I gave it Helen,
    I bade her, if her fortunes ever stood
    Necessitied to help, that by this token   85
    I would relieve her. Had you that craft to reave her
    Of what should stead her most?
Ber.   My gracious sovereign,
    Howe'er it pleases you to take it so,
    The ring was never hers.
Count.   Son, on my life,
    I've seen her wear it; and she reckon'd it   90
    At her life's rate.
Laf.   I'm sure I saw her wear it.
Ber. You are deceiv'd, my lord, she never saw it:
    In Florence was it from a casement thrown me,
    Wrapp'd in a paper, which contain'd the name
    Of her that threw it. Noble she was, and thought   95
    I stood ingag'd: but when I had subscrib'd
    To mine own fortune, and inform'd her fully
    I could not answer in that course of honour

---

90. *I've*] Pope, *I have* Ff.   91. *life's*] Rowe, *liues* Ff; *I'm*] Pope, *I am* Ff.
96. *ingag'd*] *engaged* Rowe.

83.] Elze compares the supposed gift of a ring by Elizabeth to Essex, when the latter sailed for Cadiz, 1596 (cf. *Henry VIII.*). "In Samuel Rowley's *When you see me, you know me*, there is a similar giving of a ring" (Hunter).

84. *I bade her*] an elliptical construction. To make it quite clear, understand "I bade her . . . (remember) that by this token . . ."

85. *Necessitied*] in need of help.

96. *ingag'd*] not gaged (not ingaged). Cf. inhabitable = uninhabitable. Also *Merchant of Venice*, I. i. 130, where the positive "gaged" is used.

96. *subscrib'd*] given an account of.

As she had made the overture, she ceas'd
In heavy satisfaction, and would never 100
Receive the ring again.
King. Plutus himself,
That knows the tinct and multiplying medicine,
Hath not in nature's mystery more science
Than I have in this ring : 'twas mine, 'twas Helen's
Whoever gave it you. Then, if you know 105
That you are well acquainted with yourself,
Confess 'twas hers, and by what rough enforcement
You got it from her. She call'd the saints to surety,
That she would never put it from her finger,
Unless she gave it to yourself in bed, 110
Where you have never come, or sent it us
Upon her great disaster.
Ber. She never saw it.
King. Thou speak'st it falsely, as I love mine honour;
And mak'st conjectural fears to come into me,
Which I would fain shut out. If it should prove 115
That thou art so inhuman,—'twill not prove so;
And yet I know not: thou didst hate her deadly,

101. *Plutus*] Rowe, *Platus* Ff. *falsely: as . . . honour,* Ff.

113. *falsely, as . . . honour;*] Rowe,

100. *heavy satisfaction*] "sadly acquiescing in what she acknowledged to be necessary" (Schmidt).
101. *Plutus*] "The grand alchemist, who knows the tincture which confers the properties of gold upon base metals, and the matter by which gold is multiplied, by which a small quantity of gold is made to communicate its qualities to a large mass of base metal." In the reign of Henry IV. a law was made to forbid all men thenceforth to multiply gold, or use any craft of multiplication. Cf. *Antony and Cleopatra*, I. v. 37, "that great medicine hath With his tinct gilded thee." The *grand elixir* of the alchemists is here referred to.
106. *That . . . yourself*] The use of "*if* you know" is similar to that in *Macbeth*, III. iv. 74, "If I stand here, I saw him." The meaning in this passage is: "As sure as you know that you are well acquainted with yourself."

And she is dead; which nothing, but to close
Her eyes myself, could win me to believe,
More than to see this ring. Take him away. 120
                    [*Guards seize Bertram.*
My fore-past proofs, howe'er the matter fall,
Shall tax my fears of little vanity,
Having vainly fear'd too little. Away with him!
We'll sift this matter further.
Ber.   If you shall prove
This ring was ever hers, you shall as easy 125
Prove that I husbanded her bed in Florence,
Where yet she never was. [*Exit, guarded.*
King. I am wrapp'd in dismal thinkings.

          Enter a Gentleman.

Gent.   Gracious sovereign,
Whether I have been to blame or no, I know
    not:
Here's a petition from a Florentine, 130
Who hath for four or five removes come short
To tender it herself. I undertook it,
Vanquish'd thereto by the fair grace and speech
Of the poor suppliant, who by this I know
Is here attending: her business looks in her 135
With an importing visage, and she told me,

---

122. *tax*] F 3, 4; *taxe* F 2; *taxe* F 1.   127. Exit, guarded] Rowe, omitted Ff.   128. Enter a Gentleman] before "I am ... thinkings" Ff.

123. *Having vainly*] "The proofs I have already known all the time are so evident that, whatever the ultimate result, my fears will have proved to have been too wavering, too feeble."

131. *removes*] day's journeys. A frequent word to describe the journeys of *parties*, such as a king and his retinue.
131. *come short*] fail to overtake.

In a sweet verbal brief, it did concern
Your highness with herself.

King. *Upon his many protestations to marry me when
his wife was dead, I blush to say it, he won me.* 140
*Now is the Count Rousillon a widower: his vows
are forfeited to me, and my honour's paid to him.
He stole from Florence, taking no leave, and I
follow him to his country for justice. Grant it
me, O king! in you it best lies; otherwise a seducer* 145
flourishes, and a poor maid is undone.
                                         DIANA CAPILET.

Laf. I will buy me a son-in-law in a fair, and toll for
    this: I'll none of him.
King. The heavens have thought well on thee, Lafeu, 150
    To bring forth this discovery. Seek these suitors:
    Go speedily and bring again the count.
                [*Exeunt Gentleman and some Attendants.*
    I am afeard the life of Helen, lady,
    Was foully snatch'd.
Count.   Now, justice on the doers!

142. honour's] Rowe; honors F 1, 2, 3; honours, F 4.   144. his country]
F 1, 2; this country F 3, 4.   148. *fair*] F 1; *fear* F 3, 4; *feare* F 2; *and
toll*] *a toule* Becket conj.   148, 149. *toll for this: I'll] toule for this. Ile* F
1; *toule him for this. Ile* F 2, 3, 4.   152. Exeunt...] Malone, omitted Ff.

137. *sweet ... brief*] To Rolfe this phrase seems exactly to describe itself and many others like it in the poet's language—condensed "sweetness and light"—"infinite riches in a little room."

148, 149. *toll for this*] "pay a tax for the liberty of selling" this=Bertram. The toll-book was ordered by law "to prevent the sale of such (horses) as were stolen and to preserve the property to the right owner." Lafeu means "I will put Bertram up for sale; I prefer to have any other." Some editors take it to mean I will toll the bell for this Bertram, get rid of him. The toll-book in which horses sold at fairs were entered is alluded to in *The Revenger's Tragedy* (*apud* Dodsley, *l.c.* x. 44). See also The play of Stuckley (*apud* Simpson, *The School of Shakespeare*, vol. ii. p. 210).

Re-enter BERTRAM, *guarded.*

King. I wonder, sir, sith wives are monsters to you, 155
And that you fly them as you swear them lordship,
Yet you desire to marry.

Re-enter Gentleman, with Widow and DIANA.

What woman's that?

Dia. I am, my lord, a wretched Florentine,
Derived from the ancient Capilet:
My suit, as I do understand, you know, 160
And therefore know how far I may be pitied.

Wid. I am her mother, sir, whose age and honour
Both suffer under this complaint we bring,
And both shall cease, without your remedy.

King. Come hither, county; do you know these women?

Ber. My lord, I neither can nor will deny 166
But that I know them: do they charge me further?

Dia. Why do you look so strange upon your wife?

Ber. She's none of mine, my lord.

Dia. If you shall marry,
You give away this hand, and that is mine; 170
You give away heaven's vows, and those are mine;
You give away myself, which is known mine;

---

154. Re-enter . . .] after line 153 in the Ff. 155. *sir, sith wives are monsters*] Dyce; *Sir, sir, wives are monsters* F 1; *Sir, wives are such monsters* F 2; *Sir, wives are so monstrous* F 3, 4. 157. Re-enter . . .] Malone; Enter Widow, Diana, and Parolles Ff. 165. *hither*] F 2, 3, 4; *hether* F 1; *county;*] Dyce (ed. 2) (S. Walker conj.), *count;* Ff.

155. *sith wives*]The Folio reads, "Sir, sir wives," which, if not absolute nonsense (it has been taken to express the king's impatience), is a very unusual phrase. Dyce's emendation sith (since) seems so plausible as to be almost a certainty.

164. *cease*] perish (as above). Both my age and honour will come to an end unless I have your remedy.

For I by vow am so embodied yours,
That she which marries you must marry me;
Either both or none. 175
Laf. Your reputation comes too short for my daughter:
you are no husband for her.
Ber. My lord, this is a fond and desperate creature,
Whom sometime I have laugh'd with; let your highness
Lay a more noble thought upon mine honour 180
Than for to think that I would sink it here.
King. Sir, for my thoughts, you have them ill to friend
Till your deeds gain them: fairer prove your honour
Than in my thought it lies.
Dia. Good my lord,
Ask him upon his oath, if he does think 185
He had not my virginity.
King. What say'st thou to her?
Ber. She's impudent, my lord;
And was a common gamester to the camp.
Dia. He does me wrong, my lord; if I were so,
He might have bought me at a common price: 190
Do not believe him. O! behold this ring,
Whose high respect and rich validity
Did lack a parallel; yet for all that
He gave it to a commoner o' the camp,
If I be one.
Count. He blushes, and 'tis hit: 195

183. *gain them: fairer*] Hanmer (Theobald conj.), *gain them fairer:* Ff.
195. *'tis hit*] *'tis it* Capell, *'tis his* Pope, *is hit* Malone conj., *'tis fit* Henley conj.

192. *validity*] worth. Cf. "more validity . . . lives in carrion flies than Romeo" (*Romeo and Juliet*, III. iii. 33).

195. *'tis hit*] 'tis found out. Cf. "Thou hast hit it" (*Taming of the Shrew*, II. 199). In most editions the emendation "'tis it" has been adopted.

Of six preceding ancestors, that gem
Conferr'd by testament to th' sequent issue,
Hath it been owed and worn. This is his wife:
That ring's a thousand proofs.

King.   Methought you said
You saw one here in court could witness it.   200

Dia. I did, my lord, but loath am to produce
So bad an instrument: his name's Parolles.

Laf. I saw the man to-day, if man he be.

King. Find him, and bring him hither.

Ber.   What of him?
He's quoted for a most perfidious slave,   205
With all the spots o' the world tax'd and debosh'd
Whose nature sickens but to speak a truth.
Am I or that or this for what he'll utter,
That will speak any thing?

King.   She hath that ring of yours

Ber. I think she has: certain it is I lik'd her,   210
And boarded her i' the wanton way of youth.
She knew her distance, and did angle for me,
Madding my eagerness with her restraint,

---

197. *to th'*] F 3, 4; *to 'th* F 1, 2.   207. *Whose . . . truth*] Hanmer, *Whose
nature sickens: but . . . truth*, Ff.   211. *boardea*] Rowe, *boorded* Ff.

197. *sequent issue*] a legal term: the next heir to whom personal property is bequeathed.
202. *instrument*] a thing or person useful as a means to an end.
205. *quoted*] cited. Cf. "A fellow by the hand of nature marked, quoted and signed to do a deed of shame" (*King John*, IV. ii. 222).
206. *debosh'd*] See above, II. iii. 140.
208. *Am I or . . .*] not to be or this or that for = to be indifferent to.

211. *boarded*] See Cotgrave: "*aborder* = to approach, accoast, abboord . . . come or draw neer unto." Cf. "Whom, thus at gaze, the palmer 'gan to board With goodly reason, and thus fair bespake" (Spenser). Also *Hamlet*, II. ii. 170, "Away, I do beseech you both, away; I'll board him presently."
213. *Madding*] the only verb in Shakespeare meaning "to make mad."

As all impediments in fancy's course
Are motives of more fancy; and, in fine, 215
Her infinite cunning, with her modern grace,
Subdued me to her rate: she got the ring,
And I had that which any inferior might
At market-price have bought.

Dia. I must be patient;
You, that have turn'd off a first so noble wife, 220
May justly diet me. I pray you yet,

216. *infinite cunning*] Singer (S. Walker conj. and Collier MS.); *insuite comming* F 1; *insuit comming* F 2, 3; *insuit coming* F 4. 218. *any*] *an* or *my* S. Walker conj. 221. *diet*] *dyet* Ff, *dye to* conj.

215. *fancy*] love; frequently used in this sense. Cf. "a martial man to be soft fancy's slave" (*Lucrece*, 200).

216. *modern grace*] Editors have found it difficult to explain this expression. Williams asks, "What are we to understand by 'modern grace'? Johnson tells us explicitly that, in Shakespeare, 'modern' has the signification of 'vulgar,' 'mean,' 'common.' Malone understands it to mean 'common,' 'ordinary'; Walker 'trivial,' 'everyday.' That such was its early meaning we may learn from this play, II. iii. 2, where we hear of 'philosophical persons, to make modern and familiar, things supernatural and causeless.' Could such an epithet be, under any circumstances, applicable to grace (it would be preposterous, in this case, to suppose an oxymoron), and, if it could, would 'modern grace' convey the evident purport of Bertram's explanation of his conduct? Assuredly not. Could Bertram wish it to be believed that he had been betrayed by a woman of but commonplace attractions? . . .." Bertram is evidently trying to excuse his conduct; probably he meant very much what Beaumont and Fletcher implied when they wrote, "Can red and white An eye, a nose, a cheek— . . . with a little turn That wanton fools call fashion thus abuse me?" (*Bonduca*, II. ii.).

217. *rate*] condition, *i.e.* the gift of the ring.

218. *any*] Walker supposes this to be a misprint; as in *Love's Labour's Lost*, I. i. 104, where "Why should I joy in any abortive birth?" is printed by mistake for "an abortive birth."

221. *diet*] undoubtedly corrupt, but nothing to replace it. Malone interprets it "may justly loath or be weary of me, as people generally are of a regimen or prescribed and scanty diet." Collins and Steevens think she means "may justly make me fast, by depriving me (as Desdemona says) of the rites for which I love you." Steevens adds that the allusion may be to the management of hawks who were half-starved till they became tractable. Thus in *Coriolanus*, "I'll watch him, Till he be dieted to my request." To fast, like one who takes diet, is a comparison that occurs in *The Two Gentlemen of Verona*. If we are to accept the reading 'diet,' it seems preferable to accept the latter interpretation, as answering to Bertram's "turning off" of Helena. Shakespeare may have written something like "do't to me" or "do't with me," or perhaps "dye to me." (See *Rom.* xiv. 7.)

                Since you lack virtue I will lose a husband,
                Send for your ring; I will return it home,
                And give me mine again.
Ber.   I have it not.
King. What ring was yours, I pray you?
Dia.   Sir, much like   225
                The same upon your finger.
King. Know you this ring? this ring was his of late.
Dia. And this was it I gave him, being abed.
King. The story then goes false, you threw it him
                Out of a casement.
Dia.   I have spoke the truth.   230

                Enter Attendant with PAROLLES.

Ber. My lord, I do confess the ring was hers.
King. You boggle shrewdly, every feather starts you.
                Is this the man you speak of?
Dia.   Ay, my lord.
King. Tell me, sirrah, but tell me true, I charge you,
                Not fearing the displeasure of your master,   235
                Which on your just proceeding I'll keep off,
                By him and by this woman here what know you?
Par. So please your majesty, my master hath been

226.] Arranged as in Capell; in one line in Ff; Hanmer would put "Sir" after "finger."   227. *ring?*] Theobald, *Ring*, Ff.

223. *home*] Cf. "So thy great gift, upon misprision growing, comes home again" (*Sonnets*, lxxxvii. 12). Also, "Now to Helen is (my heart) home returned"(*Midsummer-Night's Dream*, III. ii. 172).
232. *boggle*] change about. Antony says to Cleopatra, "you have been a boggler ever," where the context tells us that he means "a fickle woman" (*Antony and Cleopatra*, III. xiii. 110).
237. *By . . . you?*] "By" is sometimes used by Shakespeare after verbs of speaking, thinking and knowing "about." Cf. *Much Ado*, v. i. 313, "anything that I do know by her"; *Merchant of Venice*, I. ii. 58, "how say

an honourable gentleman: tricks he hath had in
him, which gentlemen have. 240

King. Come, come, to the purpose: did he love this
woman?

Par. Faith, sir, he did love her; but how?

King. How, I pray you?

Par. He did love her, sir, as a gentleman loves a woman. 245

King. How is that?

Par. He loved her, sir, and loved her not.

King. As thou art a knave, and no knave. What an
equivocal companion is this!

Par. I am a poor man, and at your majesty's com- 250
mand.

Laf. He's a good drum, my lord, but a naughty orator.

Dia. Do you know he promised me marriage?

Par. Faith, I know more than I'll speak.

King. But wilt thou not speak all thou knowest? 255

Par. Yes, so please your majesty. I did go between
them, as I said; but more than that, he loved
her, for indeed he was mad for her, and talked of
Satan, and of limbo, and of Furies, and I know
not what: yet I was in that credit with them at 260
that time, that I knew of their going to bed, and
of other motions, as promising her marriage, and

243. *but how?*] Malone thinks that this belongs to the next speech of the king.
248. *knave.*] knave, Ff. 257. *than that, he*] F 3, 4; *then that he* F 1, 2.

you by the French Lord?" Also, "For
I know nothing by (concerning) myself; yet am I not hereby justified:
but he that judgeth me is the Lord"
(1 Cor. iv. 4).

252. *naughty*] worthless (German,
nichtig). *King Lear,* II. iv. 136, "Thy
sister's naught: O Regan! she hath

. . ." Sidney wrote, "A prince of
great courage and beauty, but fostered
up in blood by his naughty father."

262. *motions*] suggestions. Cf. "I'll
join my daughter to him forthwith in
holy wedlock bands.—I thank you for
your motion" (*3 Henry VI.* III.
244).

things that would derive me ill will to speak of:
therefore I will not speak what I know.

King. Thou hast spoken all already, unless thou canst 265
say they are married: but thou art too fine in
thy evidence; therefore stand aside.
This ring, you say, was yours.

Dia.   Ay, my good lord.

King. Where did you buy it? or who gave it you?

Dia. It was not given me, nor I did not buy it.   270

King. Who lent it you?

Dia.   It was not lent me neither.

King. Where did you find it then?

Dia.   I found it not.

King. If it were yours by none of all these ways,
How could you give it him?

Dia.   I never gave it him.

Laf. This woman's an easy glove, my lord: she goes 275
off and on at pleasure.

King. This ring was mine: I gave it his first wife.

Dia. It might be yours or hers, for aught I know.

King. Take her away; I do not like her now.
To prison with her; and away with him.   280
Unless thou tell'st me where thou hadst this ring
Thou diest within this hour.

Dia.   I 'll never tell you.

---

270. *nor I did not*] F 1, 2; *nor did not* F 3, 4.   278. *aught*] Theobald (ed. 2), *ought* Ff.

263. *derive me ill*] bring down ill on me. Cf. "What friend of mine that had to him derived your anger, did I continue in my liking?" (*Henry VIII.* II. iv. 32).

266. *fine*] subtle. Cf. "The finest mad devil of jealousy" (*Merry Wives*, v. i. 19).

270. *nor I did not*] one of the double negatives so common in Elizabethan literature.

King. Take her away.
Dia. I'll put in bail, my liege.
King. I think thee now some common customer.
Dia. By Jove, if ever I knew man, 'twas you. 285
King. Wherefore hast thou accus'd him all this while?
Dia. Because he's guilty, and he is not guilty.
  He knows I am no maid, and he'll swear
    to 't:
  I'll swear I am a maid, and he knows not.
  Great king, I am no strumpet, by my life; 290
  I'm either maid, or else this old man's wife.
King. She does abuse our ears: to prison with her!
Dia. Good mother, fetch my bail. [*Exit Widow.*
                    Stay, royal sir:
  The jeweller that owes the ring is sent for,
  And he shall surety me. But for this lord, 295
  Who hath abus'd me, as he knows himself,
  Though yet he never harm'd me, here I quit
    him:
  He knows himself my bed he hath defil'd,
  And at that time he got his wife with child:
  Dead though she be, she feels her young one
    kick: 300
  So there's my riddle: one that's dead is quick;
  And now behold the meaning.

291. *I'm*] Pope, *I am* Ff.   293. Exit Widow] Pope, omitted Ff.

288. *knows*] "'To know' seems to be used in more than one passage of this play in the sense of *opinari*, as its sister γνῶναι sometimes is" (S. Walker, *Crit. Ex.* iii. 81).
 294. *jeweller*] "Jewellers were formerly the only bankers, and being therefore considered wealthy, were unexceptionable bail" (H. T.).
 294. *owes*] possesses, as above.
 297. *quit him*] declare him to be quit. Cf. "God quit you in his mercy" (*Henry V.* II. ii. 166).

Re-enter Widow with HELENA.

King. Is there no exorcist
Beguiles the truer office of mine eyes?
Is't real that I see?

Hel. No, my good lord;
'Tis but the shadow of a wife you see; 305
The name and not the thing.

Ber. Both, both. O! pardon.

Hel. O my good lord! when I was like this maid,
I found you wondrous kind. There is your ring;
And, look you, here's your letter; this it says:
When from my finger you can get this ring, 310
And are by me with child, etc.
This is done:
Will you be mine, now you are doubly won?

Ber. If she, my liege, can make me know this clearly,
I'll love her dearly, ever, ever dearly.

Hel. If it appear not plain and prove untrue, 315
Deadly divorce step between me and you!
O! my dear mother; do I see you living?

Laf. Mine eyes smell onions; I shall weep anon.
[*To Parolles.*] Good Tom Drum, lend me a handkercher: so, I thank thee. Wait on me home, 320
I'll make sport with thee: let thy courtesies
alone, they are scurvy ones.

302. Re-enter . . .] Capell; Enter Hellen and Widow Ff. 303. *truer office*] *true Office* F 3, *true Officer* F 4. 311. are] Rowe, is Ff. 319. [To Parolles] Rowe, omitted F. 319, 320. *Good . . . handkercher*] as verse in Ff. 321. *courtesies*] *curtsies* Ff.

302. *exorcist*] here used in the sense of *Witchcraft*, Bk. XV. ii., "to raise a of one who *raises* spirits, by no ghost . . . the exorcist must seek out means usual. Cf. Scott, *The Discovery* . . ." (W. J. C., *Little Quarto Shak.*).

King. Let us from point to point this story know,
    To make the even truth in pleasure flow.
    [*To Diana.*] If thou be'st yet a fresh uncropped
        flower, 325
    Choose thou thy husband, and I'll pay thy dower;
    For I can guess that by thy honest aid
    Thou kept'st a wife herself, thyself a maid.
    Of that and all the progress, more and less,
    Resolvedly more leisure shall express: 330
    All yet seems well; and if it end so meet,
    The bitter past, more welcome is the sweet.
                                 [*Flourish.*

---

325. [To Diana] Rowe, omitted Ff.   328. *kept'st*] *keptst* F 1; *keeptst* F 2; *keepest* F 3, 4.   330. *Resolvedly*] F 4, *Resoldvedly* F 1; *Resoldv'dly* F 2, 3.

324. *even truth*] whole truth. Cf. "The king hath run bad humours on the knight; that's the even of it" (*Henry V.* II. i. 128). There is a shade of meaning in it which connects it with the verb "flow" that follows.

330. *Resolvedly*] until all is resolved or explained. Cf. "at pick'd leisure... single I'll resolve you... of every These happen'd accidents" (*Tempest*, v. i. 248).

[EPILOGUE.

EPILOGUE

Spoken by the KING.

The king's a beggar, now the play is done:
All is well ended, if this suit be won,
That you express content; which we will pay,
With strife to please you, day exceeding day:
Ours be your patience then, and yours our parts;   5
Your gentle hands lend us, and take our hearts.

[*Exeunt.*

Epilogue . . . King] Pope.

1. The king's a beggar] Reference to the Ballad. In *Love's Labour's Lost* Armado asks his page, "Is there not a ballad, boy, of the King and the Beggar?" To which Moth replies, "The world was very guilty of such a ballad some three ages since; but, I think, now 'tis not to be found; or, if it were, it would neither serve for the writing nor the time." In spite of which remarks it has been looked for and found, Rolfe says, in Percy's *Reliques*. Cf. *Richard II*. v. iii. 80, "Our scene is altered from a serious thing, And now changed to 'The Beggar and the King.'"

4. day . . . day] every day better than the day before.

5. Ours be . . . and yours] Let us have your patience, you will have our parts, our acting.

CPSIA information can be obtained
at www.ICGtesting.com
Printed in the USA
LVOW10s2325190318
570450LV00010B/406/P